DIVIDING THE AS FAMILY BREAKDOWN

DIVIDING THE ASSETS ON FAMILY BREAKDOWN

Edited by
Professor Rebecca Bailey-Harris MA, BCL
Faculty of Law, University of Bristol

Family Law
1998

Published by
Family Law
a publishing imprint of
Jordan Publishing Limited
21 St Thomas Street
Bristol BS1 6JS

© Jordan Publishing Limited 1998

All rights reserved. No part of this publication may be
reproduced, stored in a retrieval system, or transmitted in
any way or by any means, including photocopying or recording,
without the written permission of the copyright holder,
application for which should be addressed to the publisher.

British Library Cataloguing-in-Publication Data

A catalogue record for this book is available
from the British Library.

ISBN 0 85308 529 3

Photoset by Mendip Communication Ltd, Frome, Somerset
Printed in Great Britain by MPG Books Ltd, Bodmin, Cornwall

INTRODUCTION

This book has its genesis in a seminar which took place on 21 March 1998 at King's College, University of London, under the auspices of the Society of Public Teachers of Law. The Society has adopted 'Strengths and Weaknesses of the Law' as the theme for its seminar programme over a three-year period. The aim is to explore the merits and defects of English law with the benefit of comparative perspectives. The first seminar to take place in the programme was at King's College which took as its title 'Dividing the Assets on Family Breakdown'. The topic was deliberately broad in definition, embracing distribution of assets on the breakdown of both marriage and less formalised relationships. One aim was to ask whether the policy issues underpinning breakdown should be common or distinct.

The seminar was addressed by six speakers, three from the UK and three from overseas, and was attended by some thirty other participants who made valuable contributions to the debate.

What issues are foremost in the current debate on asset distribution on family breakdown in the countries represented at the seminar? Considering marriage breakdown first, it might be thought that the overall objective of private law was relatively uncontroversial: to achieve a fair adjustment between the parties. But beyond that generalisation, a far greater degree of controversy emerges in respect of the content of fairness, and in balancing the interests of adults and children when they compete. Should the law simply recognise, arguably as a logical consequence of the adoption of irretrievable breakdown of marriage as the basis for divorce, that parties must adjust to the financial consequences and to what may be a drastic change in their respective positions? Or should the law aim to equalise, between husband and wife, the economic effects of marriage and its breakdown? A consequential issue is the means by which the law's policy should be realised, and whether the same or different considerations should govern the distribution of property and of income. A central debate has been that between rule equality, embodied in a principle of equal division of matrimonial property, and equality of result or outcome, which requires a further adjustment to take account of the impact of the marriage on the parties' financial positions. Which of these better reflects the concept of marriage as a common endeavour? Also controversial is the role of spouse maintenance: is it an undesirable indicator of dependency or a legitimate means of realising the right to the equalisation of the economic effects of marriage? Broader questions arise as to the role of legal regulation of the family and its breakdown. The interests of state paternalism and party autonomy may conflict; the focus for this debate is currently the vigorous promotion in many parts of the world of private ordering as the preferred means of dispute resolution. Linked to this is the extent to which the state has an interest in preserving the public purse.

Chapters 1, 2 and 3 address these issues from the perspectives of three different legal systems. Lord Justice Thorpe evaluates the English system of ancillary relief which currently vests a high degree of discretion in the courts and gives flexible powers to distribute a pool of assets in the light of a wide range of statutory considerations. Chapter 2 examines the strengths and weaknesses of the Australian approach under Part VIII of the Family Law Act 1975 (Cth). Australia also adopts the discretionary model, although there are significant differences of detail and policy, including a greater delineation of entitlement to property division and to spouse maintenance respectively. Peter Nygh evaluates not only the current operation of the law but also the debate which has occurred in Australia in recent years over the direction of future reforms, including a possible move to greater structuring of discretion and whether taking violence into account in asset readjustment is compatible with no-fault divorce. Horst Lücke's paper analyses, from a civilist's perspective, the matrimonial property regimes operating in Germany, which provide an interesting contrast to the common law tradition. The applicable regime may either be that imposed by the general law (various forms of deferred community of property and equalisation of accrued gains) or that chosen by the spouses; German law thus respects the interests of both party autonomy and state paternalism. The approaches adopted in German law arguably reflect the concept of marriage as a common endeavour and the impossibility of evaluating, on its breakdown, the precise value of the different contributions made by each spouse.

Two specific issues are currently prominent in the debate on legal regulation of the financial consequences of marriage breakdown. One is the respective merits of wide judicial discretion and more structured rules as the means of effecting asset readjustment. The competing considerations are not only ideological but also practical: how to reconcile competing considerations of clarity, certainty and predictability with the need to do justice in the individual case. This debate is fuelled in the current economic and political climate by the desire to cut the costs of civil justice both to the litigant and to the taxpayer. Chapters 1, 2 and 3 bring very different perspectives to bear on this issue. English law is an example of a very wide discretion. Australia has traditionally adopted the same model but in recent years has struggled, both through case-law and through legislative proposals, to structure the exercise of discretion. In Germany, the community of property approach appears far more formalistic, but, as Chapter 3 explains, the details of the general regimes coupled with the ability of spouses to contract for themselves in reality renders the overall picture far more complex. The second specific issue is how pension entitlements can be taken into account in the overall distribution of assets on divorce. There is no doubt whatever that pensions represent a very significant resource for many couples.

Yet the problem of their treatment in the context of divorce is a complex one, not only on account of the nature of the expectation and the difficulty of valuation but also in identifying the basis of entitlement, in particular, the relationship with the general principles of the law governing asset distribution. German law has an established tradition of pension-splitting but treats this asset as *sui generis* meriting a tailor-made solution of its own. The United Kingdom and Australia are just beginning to tackle the problem of pension-splitting. Proposals for new legislation in England are much further advanced than in Australia, as Chapters 2 and 4 disclose. Robin Ellison provides in Chapter 4 a detailed analysis of the practical problems and a critique of the proposed solutions in the United Kingdom.

The two concluding chapters of this book address the legal regulation of the breakdown of families outside marriage. Frances Olsen takes a United States perspective, and Rebecca Bailey-Harris critically evaluates the current state of English law in the light of recent developments in Australia. In this field, the very objective of legal regulation is controversial; in particular, it is difficult to reconcile the competing claims of diversity and paternalism in contemporary society. It is possible to identify objectives of the law which are common to the breakdown of both marriage and less formal relationships, such as the just distribution of assets in recognition of the value of different contributions made to a common endeavour, and the equalisation of the economic effects of the relationship. But the problem is how to realise those objectives without seriously undermining diversity and self-determination by forcing parties into models of legal institutions which they have deliberately avoided. One formidable issue is the sheer diversity of family relationships which lie beyond the boundary of the marriage certificate. Differences lie not only in sexuality and the significance of sexual relations, but also in duration and the parties' expectations of the relationship. How should the relationship to which legal protection attaches be defined? Does diversity in family form demand diversity in legal consequences? Should the state attach more weight to party autonomy in the case of the unmarried than the married? Chapters 5 and 6 explore these issues. In the past, the reluctance of the state to regulate relationships outside marriage has been explained against the background of the current moral climate and the fear of undermining the sanctity of marriage – an approach which, controversially, has recently resurfaced in the current climate of 'family values' discourse. The case for reform in this field, which to many seems unarguable, has proved surprisingly difficult to advance.

The seminar and this book are timely, since the future direction of the law governing asset distribution on the breakdown of both marriage and other relationships is currently on the discussion table in this country. The government is, at the time of writing, floating proposals for the introduction of some new principles into ancillary relief under Part II of the Matrimonial Causes Act 1973, namely a possible presumption of equal division of matrimonial property and greater recognition for pre-nuptial contracts. Publication of The Law Commission's discussion of homesharers is long awaited. It is hoped that this book will help to stimulate the debate. As convenor of the seminar, it remains only for me to thank the speakers who gave so generously of their time and scholarship, the Chairman, and Peter Niven, the Administrative Secretary of the Society of Public Teachers of Law who most ably carried out the practical organisation.

Rebecca Bailey-Harris
Bristol, September 1998

SPEAKERS

The Right Honourable Lord Justice Thorpe is a Lord Justice of the Court of Appeal and an expert in family law. He chairs many committees including the Lord Chancellor's Advisory Group on Ancillary Relief.

The Honourable Dr Peter Nygh was formerly a judge of the Appeal Division of the Family Court of Australia and a Professor of Law at Macquarie University and is currently an Adjunct Professor at the University of New South Wales.

Professor Horst Lücke was formerly Professor of Law at the University of Adelaide and is currently Research Associate at the Max-Planck-Institut für auslandisches u. internationales Privatrecht in Hamburg.

Mr Robin Ellison is a solicitor, author and National Head of Pensions at Eversheds in London; he is one of the country's leading experts on pensions in family law.

Professor Rebecca Bailey-Harris was formerly an academic in Australia and a part-time member of the Australian Law Reform Commission prior to taking up a chair at the University of Bristol and joining the Lord Chancellor's Advisory Group on Ancillary Relief.

Professor Frances Olsen is Professor at the University of California, Los Angeles and at the time of the seminar was Visiting Fellow at Churchill College, Cambridge. She is internationally recognised as a leading feminist scholar.

Revised versions of each of the papers presented form Chapters 1 to 6 of this book. The seminar was chaired by Professor Nigel Lowe, Director of the Centre for International Family Law Studies at Cardiff Law School.

CONTENTS

Introduction	v
Speakers	ix
Table of Cases	xv

Chapter 1   THE ENGLISH SYSTEM OF ANCILLARY RELIEF
The Rt Hon Lord Justice Thorpe   1

Chapter 2   ASSET DISTRIBUTION ON BREAKDOWN OF MARRIAGE IN AUSTRALIA
The Hon Dr Peter Nygh   11

Introduction	11
The process of property division	12
What is 'property'?	13
The assessment of contributions	18
Matrimonial property reform	21
The need for reform	21
General principles of property division	22
Financial agreements and pre-nuptial agreements	25
Superannuation	26
Conclusion	27

Chapter 3   DIVIDING THE ASSETS ON FAMILY BREAKDOWN: THE GERMAN CIVIL CODE
Professor Horst Lücke   29

Introduction	29
I. Family breakdown: division of property under matrimonial property regimes	31
1. The separation of goods and the community of property regime	32
2. The community of accrued gains	33
II. Family breakdown: adjustment of pension entitlements	40
1. Pensions: a complex and vitally important part of the 'social net'	40
2. Pensions: legislative options	41
III. Unmarried relationships (URs): division of property on breakdown	50
1. The constitutional dimensional	50
2. The public policy dimension	51

		3. The case for legal intervention after the break-up of URs	52
	IV.	The German system: some personal views	54
		1. Marriage	54
		2. Unmarried relationships	55

Chapter 4   STRENGTHS AND WEAKNESSES OF THE LAW ON PENSION SPLITTING IN THE UNITED KINGDOM
Robin Ellison   57

Introduction   57
The UK pension system   58
     State benefits   58
     Occupational and personal pensions   59
     Money purchase and final salary   59
     Funded and unfunded schemes   60
     Discretionary and indexed benefits   60
Valuation   61
     Introduction   61
     Methods available   61
     Cash equivalent transfer value   62
Jurisdiction of the court   63
     Protective trusts   63
     Obtaining information   64
     Making the spouse a scheme member – the *Brooks* case   64
     The changes   65
Problems with the valuation   66
     Variability of valuations   66
     Negotiating a set-off   67
     Tax   67
     Discount for cash   67
     Discount for early payment   67
     Discount for risk   67
     Setting-off of own pension arrangements   67
     Pensions for house and 'grave hardship' practice   67
     Earmarking   67
The present system in practice   68
     Earmarking and pre-Pensions Act divorces   68
     Orders available   69
     Application for an earmarking order   69
     After the order is made   70
Conclusion   70

Chapter 5   DIVIDING THE ASSETS ON BREAKDOWN OF RELATIONSHIPS OUTSIDE MARRIAGE: CHALLENGES FOR REFORMERS
Professor Rebecca Bailey-Harris   73

	Introduction	73
	The current law	74
	Strengths of the current law	75
	Formal neutrality as to family form, gender and sexuality	75
	Flexibility	75
	Moral basis	75
	Party autonomy	76
	Weaknesses of the current law	76
	Complexity and uncertainty, resulting in lack of clarity and inaccessibility	76
	Need to prove intention to create a constructive trust	80
	Trust law gives inadequate recognition of non-financial contributions to the relationship	81
	Law operates with gender-bias in practice	81
	Inadequate consideration of future needs	82
	Inadequate consideration of future resources and the 'new property'	82
	Challenges for the direction of future reforms	83
	Party autonomy versus state paternalism	83
	Should the content of the law differ from or mirror that applying on marriage breakdown?	83
	The definition of the relationship	84
	The content of reformed principles of asset distribution	85
Chapter 6	ASSET DISTRIBUTION AFTER UNMARRIED COHABITATION: A UNITED STATES PERSPECTIVE	
	Professor Frances Olsen	89
	Introduction	89
	I. A diversity of approaches	90
	A. The 'traditional' approach of Illinois	91
	B. The partial apparent reform of Minnesota	94
	C. Enforcing actual agreements only	95
	D. The *Marvin* approach of California	97
	II. Subverting marriage?	100
	III. Alternative assumptions	101
	IV. Conclusions	102

TABLE OF CASES

References in the right-hand column are to page numbers.

ENGLAND AND WALES
Beach v Beach [1995] 2 FLR 160   76
Brooks v Brooks [1996] AC 375, [1995] 3 All ER 257, [1995] 3 WLR 141, [1995] 3 FCR 214, [1995] 2 FLR 13, [1995] Fam Law 545, [1995] *Pensions Law Reports* 173, HL   64-65
Burns v Burns [1984] Ch 317, [1984] 2 WLR 582, (1984) 14 Fam Law 244   79, 82
Conran v Conran [1997] 2 FLR 615   18
Dart v Dart [1996] 2 FLR 286   2
Drake v Whipp [1996] 1 FLR 826   76, 80
Edgar v Edgar (1981) 2 FLR 19   8
F v F (Ancillary Relief: Substantial Assets) [1995] 2 FLR 45   8, 76
Gissing v Gissing [1971] AC 886   77, 80
Grant v Edwards [1986] 3 WLR 114   78, 79, 80
H v M (Property: Beneficial Interest) [1992] 1 FLR 229   80
Lloyds Bank v Rosset [1991] AC 107   77, 78-79, 80, 82
Midland Bank v Cooke [1995] 2 FLR 915   75, 78, 80, 81
Pettitt v Pettitt [1970] AC 777   80
Practice Direction: Ancillary Relief Procedure: Pilot Scheme [1996] 2 FLR 368   8
Practice Direction: Ancillary Relief Procedure: Pilot Scheme [1997] 2 FLR 304   8
Wachtel v Wachtel [1973] Fam 72   81
Wayling v Jones [1995] 2 FLR 1029   75, 79, 82

AUSTRALIA
Ascot Investments Pty Ltd v Harper (1981) 148 CLR 337   14
Bailey, Re (1990) FLC 92-117   16
Baumgartner v Baumgartner (1987) 164 CLR 137   81
BP Australia Ltd v Amann Aviation Ltd (1996) 137 ALR 447   20
Clauson v Clauson (1994) 18 Fam LR 693   12, 13
Coulter v Coulter (1990) 13 Fam LR 421   15, 19
Crapp v Crapp, In the Marriage of Crapp (1979) 5 Fam LR 47   15, 21
Doherty v Doherty (1995) 20 Fam LR 137   20
Duff v Duff (1977) FLC 90-217   13
Elsey v Elsey (1996) 21 Fam LR 249   23
Evans v Marmont (1997) 21 Fam LR 760   86
Ferraro v Ferraro (1992) 16 Fam LR 1, (1993) FLC 92-335   12, 18, 21, 24
Fisher v Fisher (1986) 13 Fam LR 806   20
Gould v Gould (1995) 20 Fam LR 1   12
Hannah v Hannah (1989) FLC 92-052   17
Harrison v Harrison (1996) 20 Fam LR 322   15
Jones v Skinner (1835) 5 LJ Ch 90   13
Kennon v Kennon (1997) 22 Fam LR 1   20-21

McMahon v McMahon (1995) 19 Fam LR 99	12
McLay v McLay (1995) 20 Fam LR 239	12, 19, 24
Mallet v Mallet (1984) 156 CLR 605	18, 19, 22
Marsh v Marsh (1993) 17 Fam LR 289	20
Muschinski v Dodds (1985) 160 CLR 583	81
Norbis v Norbis (1986) 65 ALR 12	12
Olliver v Olliver (1978) 32 FLR 129	12
O'Shea and O'Shea [1998] FLC 91-964	15
Soblusky v Soblusky (1976) 12 ALR 699	20
Wardman v Hudson (1978) 5 Fam LR 889	18
Webber v Webber (1985) 10 Fam LR 505	15
West and Green, In the Marriage of (1991) 16 Fam LR 811	15, 16

CANADA

Pettkus v Becker (1980) 117 DLR (3d) 257	81

USA

Baehr v Lewin, 74 Haw 530; 852 P 2d 44 (1993)	89, 90
Carnes v Sheldon, 311 NW 2d 747 (Mich Ct App 1981)	96
Chaachou v Chaachou, 135 So 2d 206 (Fla 1961)	98
Greer v Richmond, 369 Mass 47, 337 NE 2d 691 (1975)	97
Hewitt v Hewitt, 62 Ill App 3d 861, 20 Ill Dec 476, 380 NE 2d 454; 77 Ill 2d 49; 394 NE 2d 1204 (1979)	91-93, 99
Jones v Daly, 176 Cal Rptr 130 (1981)	93
Kellard v Kellard, 13 Fam L Rep (BNA) 1490 (NY Sup Ct 1987)	96
Latham v Latham, 274 Or 421, 547 P 2d 144 (1976)	97
Marvin v Marvin, 18 Cal 3d 660; 557 P 2d 106; 134 Cal Rptr 815 (1976); 5 Mam L Rep 3077 (Super Ct of Calif 1979), 122 Cal App 3d 871, 176 Cal Rptr 551 (1981)	89, 90, 91, 97-100, 103
Rehak v Mathia, 238 SE 2d 81 (Ga 1977)	91
Schwegmann v Schwegmann, 441 So 2d 316 (La Ct App 1983)	93
Spafford v Coats, 118 Ill App 3d 566, 455 NE 2d 241 (1983)	93
Sparrow v Sparrow, 93 So 2d 232 (La 1957)	94
Thomson v Thomson, 236 Mo App 1223, 163 SW 2d 792 (1942)	96
Tyranski v Piggins, 44 Mich App 570, 205 NW 2d 595 (1973)	97
Wallace v Rappleye, 103 Ill 229 (1882)	91
Whorton v Dillingham, 248 Cal Rptr 405 (1988)	93

Chapter 1

THE ENGLISH SYSTEM OF ANCILLARY RELIEF

The Rt Hon Lord Justice Thorpe

Edmund Burke wrote: 'You can never plan the future by the past'.[1] Generalisations are dangerous and since in 1998 our jurisdiction is debating the reform of the statutory code for dividing the assets on family breakdown contained in the Matrimonial Causes Act 1973 it is helpful to remind ourselves of the evolution leading to the present statute. Genesis is dated 1857[2] and the court's powers in the 19th century to order financial provision were of the narrowest and reflected general legal principles including restrictions on a woman's ability to own property or to contract in her own right. Emerging from an ecclesiastical system there was a heavy emphasis on sin and guilt. In a patriarchal society, rights were for men and burdens for women. This state of affairs persisted just into this century when the carnage of the first world war lent great impetus to the movement for women's rights. Statutory reform always lags far behind social change. But the gradual progress of women towards independence and equal rights in a male dominated society had to be matched by the development of a statutory code for the division of assets post divorce and for the provision of financial security for the vulnerable. Since the present writer was called to the Bar the emphasis switched from the power to vary post- and ante-nuptial settlements and the power to order secured provision to the power to order lump sum which arrived in 1963.[3] The social conditions in which men held sway also depended upon a completely different pattern of wealth distribution. The wealth of the nation was held by a much smaller percentage of the population. Those who had it regulated it by the extensive use of settlements. The Victorian patriarch endeavoured to defy the comparative brevity of the average span by tying up family assets until the last trump. Only the rule against perpetuities[4] restricted the handiwork of the draughtsman in Lincoln's Inn. The social order seemed secure and landed estates might be expected to endure, even if coal did not lie deep beneath the plough. The only respectable investments were consols and gilts. 2½% yield and zero inflation rendered capital appreciation an unnecessary increment. There was always the risk of a black sheep but hopefully entails and heirloom

---

1   Letter to a Member of the National Assembly, 1791, p 73.
2   Matrimonial Causes Act 1857.
3   Matrimonial Causes Act 1963, s 5.
4   See Burn, *Cheshire and Burn's Modern Law of Real Property* 15th edn (Butterworths, 1994), pp 283–333.

settlements would ensure survival. Then there were the marriage settlements without which no respectable union could be consecrated at the altar. Thus it was and the statutes reflected the times.

The arrival of the lump sum in 1963 received a cautious response from the judiciary. It is not always easy to predict the reception that a statutory reform will receive. Practitioners may be slow to adjust and judges may be conservative in their interpretation. So it was with lump sums and the great reform of the writer's professional life has been, of course, the Matrimonial Proceedings and Property Act 1970 which came into force on 1 January 1971. Here was the essential tool required to work the new material, namely a society in which divorce had shed its stigma and become the norm, a society battered by so much and so rapid change that nothing seemed likely to endure, save perhaps injustice and death. Marriages were as easily dissolved as contracted. Some of the public's idols almost achieved double figures within their sexually active years. Inflation was rampant and money could be swiftly made and swiftly lost in years of boom and bust. England and Wales were no longer a sceptred isle but an increasingly attractive haven for a cosmopolitan plutocracy who paid little tax anywhere but who acquired the right to invoke the provisions of the Divorce Reform Act 1969 and the Matrimonial Causes Act 1973 after a relatively brief residential qualification. Only a jurisdiction to order the equitable redistribution of assets in the exercise of a judicial discretion could meet the challenges of changing times.

Judicial decisions over a span of approximately 10 years commencing in 1973 told us how the statutory code contained in s 25 of the Matrimonial Causes Act 1973 was to be interpreted and applied. Most of the authoritative judgments were delivered by Ormrod LJ and the present writer has endeavoured to review them in *Dart v Dart*.[5] But there were fierce criticisms of the statute. The men fought back. It was said that the statute gave women a meal ticket for life. The judicial construction that held that conduct played no part in the discretionary adjudication was painted as a charter for the shallow gold digger (female of course) who might flit from bed to bed acquiring lucrative awards from simple judges as she progressed. So came the 1984 amendments[6] introducing into the statutory check-list of criteria conduct insofar as it would be inequitable to disregard it and imposing upon the court the duty to find a clean break if that could be achieved without hardship.[7] At the same time the unrealistic statutory objective of the 1970 Act was abandoned.[8] It is to be noted that these statutory adjustments reflected social reaction to the statute and experience of its early years of trial. The 'Matrimonial Causes Act Mark II' has

---

5   [1996] 2 FLR 286.
6   Matrimonial Proceedings and Property Act 1984, s 3, inserting a new s 25(2)(g) into the Matrimonial Causes Act 1973.
7   Ibid.
8   The minimal loss principle: see Cretney and Masson *Principles of Family Law*, 6th edn (Sweet & Maxwell, 1997), pp 425–427.

now had 14 years of trial by use. How has it performed? Does it need further adjustment to reflect either experience or social change?

In 1973, The Law Commission published a proposal for a community regime limited to the matrimonial home.[9] That seemingly attracted little support. Then in 1988, the Institute of Fiscal Studies published a report 'Property and Marriage: An Integrated Approach'. In its essence the proposal was for a community of property system. In the same year, The Law Commission published *Family Law: Matrimonial Property*.[10] This report rejected a system of community of property largely on the grounds of its restrictive inflexibility. In 1991, The Law Society published a memorandum *Maintenance and Capital Provision on Divorce* which contained recommendations for statutory reform made by its Family Law Committee. The introduction recorded that the initiative had been prompted by widespread dissatisfaction among both solicitors and the public at a system which, although embodying the flexibility to deal with the circumstances of each case, was seen by many as inconsistent and lacking in certainty. The factors within the statutory check-list and the fact that no one factor held priority over any other made it impossible for a solicitor to give a definite answer to a client who asked either 'How much will I get?' or 'How much will I pay?'. The memorandum resulted from research on comparable systems, such as those in Australia, New Zealand, Germany, Sweden, Scotland and some parts of America. The system that most attracted the committee was the system enacted by the Family Law (Scotland) Act 1985. However, in the end, the committee rejected the case for complete reform:

> 'Although the committee recognises the problems inherent in the current law it does not consider that the wholesale adoption of any of the alternative systems discussed would embody sufficient advantages over the current system such as to justify a departure from it.'[11]

The committee's proposal was to maintain the existing discretionary system whilst reducing the scope of judicial discretion by introducing:

(1) pension splitting;
(2) a recognition of marriage contracts;
(3) the introduction of a formula for calculating child maintenance.

The third has already been achieved,[12] the first will soon be achieved[13] and recognition of marriage contracts is under ministerial consideration.[14] With the

---

9   Law Com No 52 *First Report on Family Property: A New Approach*; see Cretney and Masson, supra, pp 227–231.
10 Law Com No 175.
11 Memorandum *Maintenance and Capital Provision on Divorce* (The Law Society, May 1991), para 2.39.
12 Child Support Act 1991.
13 See *Pension Sharing on Divorce: Reforming Pensions for a Fairer Future* (DSS, June 1998), see also Chapter 4, infra.
14 The Lord Chancellor's Advisory Group on Ancillary Relief has been asked to express its views on the matter by 31 July 1998.

advantage of hindsight the Family Law Committee of The Law Society is entitled to commendation for the realism and prescience of its proposals.[15]

In the late 1980s and early 1990s, judges and the most experienced practitioners were voicing anger and concern at the incidence of costs in ancillary relief litigation. Highlight cases were reported in which the senseless conduct of the litigation resulted in costs that exceeded the sum in dispute by several hundred per cent. The dissatisfaction was unqualified: judges, barristers, solicitors and academics recognised that this abuse could not be allowed to continue. The more knowledgeable the individuals the profounder the concerns. This led to the formation of an ad hoc group whose first, and now historic, meeting took place in July 1992 in the room of the Senior District Judge at the Principal Registry of the Family Division in London. The group was in no doubt that the abuse could be eliminated without primary legislation but the Family Proceedings Rules Committee had essentially concerned itself with the rules necessary to implement the Children Act 1989 and an endeavour to move on to debate the reform of the rules governing the preparation of ancillary relief litigation was effectively blocked by the Lord Chancellor's Department. Whatever may be the composition of the Rules Committee the Lord Chancellor carries a right of veto. The history of the work of the group and the slow turning of the tide from scepticism to active support and encouragement from the Department have been recorded.[16] Well before the Lord Chancellor adopted the group as his own, the opposition from those within the Rules Division, which seemed to stem from the well known anxiety that proposals for change from lawyers and judges might involve the Treasury in extra costs, were overcome. But not so completely overcome that the Department would move forward without an elaborate pilot. Of course the tide for procedural reform in ancillary relief was running beside the ampler tide for civil justice reform advocated by Lord Woolf.[17] Between these two endeavours there is some inter-relationship. There is also inter-relationship between the pilot scheme and the passage of the Family Law Act 1996. There was some attempt to introduce into the debate ancillary relief reform although that was largely outside the scope of the Bill. However, during debate in the House of Lords, the then Lord Chancellor gave an assurance to another member of the House that if the Bill were enacted he would then refer to the Ancillary Relief Advisory Group consultation upon statutory reform to adopt the Scottish system. No such reference came during the remainder of the life of that Government and a similar inactivity marked the first 10 months of the life of the present administration. Of course the old administration was fighting for life and the new has had more important concerns.

---

15 As well as statutory reforms, the Committee proposed certain procedural reforms which are not necessary to consider for the purposes of the present discussion.
16 Thorpe LJ 'Procedural Reform in Ancillary Relief' [1996] Fam Law 376.
17 *Access To Justice: Final Report* (HMSO, July 1996).

However spring has now come with a speed and intensity that always marks a spring delayed. At a speech given to the Solicitors Family Law Association's national conference on 21 February 1998 in Blackpool, the Parliamentary Secretary, Mr Hoon, had much to say:

> 'Some of you will no doubt have seen the media reports about the work officials are undertaking on the law relating to property on divorce. It is certainly the case that we have asked officials to look again at possible ways of improving and modernising the way the law works in this area – as I have made clear in speaking to you this morning, this is a continuing process throughout the Department, and throughout the Government. We cannot sit back and let the law stand still, failing to adapt to modern needs. The Lord Chancellor and I will consider any proposal that offers a feasible and appropriate mechanism for bringing the workings of the law up to date. The press have focussed on two areas that are under consideration – and I emphasise that these are at a very early stage of consideration at present – no formal proposals have been made.
>
> The first of these is the possibility of making pre-nuptial agreements legally binding. It is instructive to note that such agreements are binding in almost all other European jurisdictions, and I can see significant advantages in taking this route here – principally in the greater degree of certainty about the ownership of property they afford couples. Anything that can be done to increase the certainty of the process, and, hopefully, therefore, to reduce the conflict involved, must, in my view, be worth pursing. Clearly, however, if we were to go down this route, much work would need to be done to ensure such agreements were workable – we would need to consider mechanisms for registration, and for ensuring that such agreements were fair and workable – not just for each spouse, but also for any third party, such as a pension provider. As I say, our thinking here is at an early stage, and, if we are to take this forward, I would certainly hope to involve the SFLA in ensuring that any scheme is workable.
>
> The second issue is the consideration of a presumption of an equal division of property on divorce. Officials are examining how well such a presumption works in other jurisdictions – principally in Scotland and in Denmark – and are looking at whether it would be possible to adopt such a concept here. A preliminary conclusion is that any move towards a presumption of equal sharing would need to be accompanied by a definition of matrimonial property – again a feature of most European jurisdictions. The advantages of a move in this direction would be similar to those for pre-nuptial agreements – more certainty and clarity for the parties. My instinct, however, is that neither equal sharing nor pre-nuptial agreements should oust the jurisdiction of the court – rather, any presumption should be rebuttable. In addition, I would not wish to see any rigid system that required a 50-50 split of each and every asset. It would, I think, be much better to allow the court to examine the assets as a whole and decide how any split should be made. The key must be to deliver a greater sense of certainty for the parties, without preventing the courts from ensuring that the outcome of cases is, as far as possible, fair and just to all concerned.'

Shortly thereafter these issues were to be referred to the Lord Chancellor's Advisory Group on Ancillary Relief for consultation. The following discussion represents the present writer's views expressed at the SPTL Seminar held at King's College London on 21 March 1998 from which this book is drawn.

How useful are comparative studies and how widely should they be drawn? The affluent nations of the world are likely to have some common social characteristics. Deteriorating commitment to a Judaeo-Christian variety of religion may enhance similarities; so too may the derivation of a legal system from the English common law root; so too may geographical proximity. But there is a relatively broad band of choice from the adoption of a full rule of community of property, with limited exceptions and limited opportunities to contract out, to a judicial discretion confined only by a statutory check-list and accumulated precedent. Variations between individual states may reflect historic influences, experience gained from trial and error or social factors peculiar to that society. The present writer doubts whether academic comparative studies should much influence the debate for change. The sustained interest in the Scottish model is natural in view of the proximity and ties between the two countries. But the reference to Denmark in Mr Hoon's speech was surprising. Denmark operates a regime of community of property deferred until termination of marriage with the option to contract out by written agreement that must be registered at a public registry.[18] This option allows considerable autonomy by the creation of several different types of separate property ownership. The adoption of such a model in this jurisdiction would be exceptionally radical and the Canadian experience suggests that the proportion of spouses that opt to contract out would render the regime of community the exception rather than the rule.

The Scottish system[19] can be seen as a hybrid between a fixed regime and a discretionary system. Its attraction to Government presumably is that the discretionary adjudication is guided by principles including equal sharing of the net value of the matrimonial property.[20] The introduction of such a principle may seem to hold out the promise of reducing the volume of cases that resort to litigation. But the litigious presumably are not necessarily contained by that principle. In the majority of cases the relevant date for the assessment of what is matrimonial property is the date of separation.[21] So there is scope to argue about property acquired before marriage, property acquired post separation and property acquired by way of inheritance or gift from a third party.[22] Then how keen should one be about a principle that periodical payments should not be awarded over a period exceeding three years?[23] Does

---

18 See Nielsen 'Family Law in Denmark' in Hamilton and Standley (eds) *Family Law in Europe* (Butterworths, 1998).
19 Family Law (Scotland) Act 1985.
20 Ibid, especially ss 8–13.
21 Ibid, s 10(3).
22 See the definition of 'matrimonial property' in the Family Law (Scotland) Act 1985, s 10(4).
23 Ibid, s 9(1)(d).

the introduction of five specific principles[24] necessarily introduce any more certainty into the exercise of predicting outcome and thus facilitating negotiation?

In 1985, Stephen Cretney wrote a critical assessment of the newly minted Scottish system in an article entitled 'Money After Divorce – The Mistakes We Have Made'.[25] Now as a member of the Lord Chancellor's Group on Ancillary Relief he has the opportunity to reassess our neighbours in the light of 14 years of trial and perhaps error. Dr Cretney has an unrivalled knowledge both of the development of family law and also of the narrower field of ancillary relief but he has been a practitioner and can see through the eyes of the practitioner. Professor Rebecca Bailey-Harris is also a member of the Group. She challenges its assumptions and offers perspectives drawn from the Australian model[26] which has so influenced the shape of the new procedures currently being piloted. Plainly, before any decision can be taken expert advice from Scotland is needed as to what, with the advantage of hindsight, are the perceived strengths and weaknesses of the system. It should not be forgotten that although the countries have so much in common it does not include a legal system. Nor should it be assumed that the relevant social factors are equal north and south of the border. Wholesale statutory reform is not achieved without a comparatively high price. The legal professions and the public have to be educated in a new system. Although Scottish experience and Scottish precedent is available for guidance, any statutory reform usually leads to a litigation surge as individuals test the boundaries of the new arrival.

What are the fundamental interests of the state in the division of property after divorce? Obviously the state has an interest in preventing individuals from avoiding their financial responsibilities and thereby casting unnecessary burden on the welfare state. Secondly society has a commitment to deliver justice and fairness in order to prevent the exploitation of the vulnerable and the oppression of the weak. A citizen is entitled to expect a fair result to a dispute whether he or she submits it to negotiation, mediation or litigation. After all the statutory development of contract law over the last 30 years aims to avoid unfair outcomes. But in the field of property division after divorce there is no reason why the state should not expect the spouses to take primary responsibility for the outcome, only intervening in those cases where the responsibility has manifestly not been discharged.

For that reason there is considerable attraction in empowering the parties to contract in anticipation of marriage, during marriage and in contemplation of divorce, provided that the contractual result is neither irresponsible nor unfair. Of course the pre-nuptial contract is open to abuse. The possessor of enormous

---

24   Ibid, s 9.
25   Freeman (ed) *Essays on Family Law* (Stevens & Co, London, 1986), p 34.
26   On the substantive Australian law and reform proposals, see Nygh's discussion in Chapter 2 infra.

inherited wealth pressurises the fiancee to contract out and independent advice can be little better than a pretence. An illustration of such a case is *F v F (Ancillary Relief: Substantial Assets)*,[27] although it is not wholly clear that that aspect of the history emerges from the report. There is then the difficulty of the unpredictability of relevant future events. Stipulations may be rendered inappropriate by unforeseen change. Either the bargain must be regularly revisited or there must be a residual judicial power to override. Finally the legislators should perhaps be cautious in investing too much hope in the mechanism; the fact that it is legislated does not mean that it will thereafter be used. Against these considerations the contract seems fit for a society in which the incidence of divorce has so much increased and the average length of marriage reduced. The nostalgic might say that this was re-introducing the marriage settlement in a modern guise. The voluntary arrangement to meet future financial needs and responsibilities would be adapted to defer the provision of the agreed sum from the date of marriage to the date of divorce. As to the mode of statutory achievement, the present writer would hesitate between introducing the contract as the presumed result or simply adding the contract as one of the statutory criteria for consideration currently contained in s 25(2) of the Matrimonial Causes Act 1973. Perhaps that might depend upon the stage at which the contract was made. Contracts made in contemplation of divorce are already presumptive of outcome.[28]

When a statute has served a social purpose for over a generation (in this case over 27 years)[29] it is wise to consider the need for change and to review the arguments for change. Family lawyers should be grateful that the Government is considering providing legislative time. However the extent of professional or public dissatisfaction with the existing model is by no means clear. The writer's estimation is that dissatisfaction stems not from the statute but from the excesses to which litigants and lawyers went in the abuse of a system which cast responsibility for and control of preparation of a case on the parties. The essence of the new procedure currently being piloted[30] is to remove responsibility and control from the vulnerable and to vest it in a court. It would be preferable to postpone any substantial reform of the statute pending fair trial under a radically revised method of operation. Socially driven needs for change are imperative and have already been achieved to reflect the growth and importance of pensions. As the post-career phase of life extends and high earners invest substantially in pension schemes, so legislation has taken the first progressive step and will soon take the next to arrive at pension splitting.[31] From the writer's perspective the next most pressing imperative is to tackle the

---

27 [1995] 2 FLR 45.
28 *Edgar v Edgar* (1981) FLR 19.
29 From the commencement of the Matrimonial Proceedings and Property Act 1970.
30 See the Practice Direction in [1996] 2 FLR 368; 'Ancillary Relief: The New Rules' [1996] Fam Law 230; [1996] Fam Law 612; 'FDR: The Pilot Scheme' [1996] Fam Law 746; Practice Direction [1997] 2 FLR 304.
31 See note 13 supra.

issue of the rights of cohabitees on the breakdown of long standing relationships.[32] That is a field in which The Law Commission is already at work.[33] No doubt the Government would say that the extent of the legal aid bill in family litigation is an imperative for change. But the present writer remains optimistic that a combination of the existing statutory charge[34] and the proposed procedural reforms[35] will make substantial redress. Litigation in this field is often driven by very deep emotional and psychological disturbance that no amount of statutory reform will eradicate. The past quarter century has demonstrated that a system of wide discretion is appropriate for a society that is hugely varied in its ingredients. Greater London is a profoundly cosmopolitan city and the scale and type of wealth from top to bottom is extraordinarily varied. This seminar takes place in an elegant room under the watchful eye of the first Duke of Wellington. What would he think of the discussion? Outrageous one suspects. What would his successor in title think of a proposal for community of property? Perhaps much the same. Then there are many racial minorities with different traditions and religions. These considerations lead one to question how practical it would be to move towards a more rigid regime. Of course the wider the discretion the harder to predict outcome, thus fuelling litigation that under a more rigid system might have been compromised. Equally the greater the discretion that is vested in the judge the greater the emphasis placed on the calibre of the judge. These cases must be determined by judges who have built up an ability to arrive at an acceptable outcome by accumulated experience as practitioners. Most of the district judges have practised as specialist solicitors in ancillary relief. The introduction of the 'ticketing system' for ancillary relief work on the circuit bench ensures that selected individuals have either previously sat as district judges or have had a specialist ancillary relief practice at the Bar. In the Family Division of the High Court there is a tendency to concentrate the burden of the ancillary relief litigation on those individuals who have manifestly the most experience. In the end perhaps the art is to maintain a balance between the flexibility necessary to create a bespoke garment to fit the shape of the individual case and the presumptions and criteria that by confining discretion permit a reliable assessment of probable outcome. There was nothing in the speech of the Parliamentary Secretary to suggest that this Government contemplates abandoning the search for that balance.

---

32 See Chapter 5 infra.
33 At the time of writing, a Discussion Paper is expected in Autumn 1998.
34 Legal Aid Act 1998, ss 11(2) and 16(6); see Bailey-Harris (ed) *The Family Lawyer's Handbook* (The Law Society, 1997), pp 193–196.
35 See note 30 supra.

Chapter 2

ASSET DISTRIBUTION ON BREAKDOWN OF MARRIAGE IN AUSTRALIA

The Hon Dr Peter Nygh

INTRODUCTION

This chapter highlights the most prominent aspects of the law on property division in Australia on the breakdown of marriage. It begins with a 'thumbnail sketch' of the current state of Australian law and then discusses some of the proposals for reform.

The current law is contained in the Family Law Act 1975 (Cth), a federal statute which provides a uniform law on the subject of matrimonial causes throughout Australia. The authority of the federal Parliament is limited, in this respect, to 'marriage' and to 'divorce and matrimonial causes' under placita (xxi) and (xxii) of the list of powers given to that Parliament in the Constitution.[1] Thus, property issues arising on the breakdown of a non-marital relationship fall within State power, as do the rights which third parties may have against one or both of the spouses. The Family Law Act 1975 (Cth) is administered by the Family Court of Australia, a federal court with original jurisdiction in all States and Territories, except Western Australia where the State Family Court of Western Australia has jurisdiction under the Act. However, the Family Court of Australia has appellate jurisdiction throughout Australia and is subject only to appeals to the High Court of Australia which requires the leave either of the Family Court (virtually never granted) or of the High Court itself (rarely granted).[2] Another special feature of the Family Law Act is that proceedings for divorce[3] and for financial relief[4] are separate actions. Commonly the divorce is pronounced long before contested property proceedings are heard and determined. Often the parties have re-partnered, and sometimes remarried, by the time of the hearing.

---

1   Commonwealth of Australia Constitution, s 51.
2   On jurisdiction and constitution of the Family Court of Australia, see the Family Law Act 1975 (Cth), Parts IV and V.
3   Family Law Act 1975 (Cth), Part VI.
4   Ibid, Part VIII.

THE PROCESS OF PROPERTY DIVISION

The relevant provision is found in s 79(1) of the Family Law Act 1975 (Cth). It authorises the court to make 'such order as it considers appropriate altering the interests of the parties in the property ... for the benefit of either or both of the parties or a child of the marriage'. Under s 79(2) the court is not to make an order 'unless it is satisfied that, in all the circumstances, it is just and equitable to make the order'. As can be seen from those provisions, the court's powers are discretionary and the exercise of that discretion will depend on the circumstances of each case.

The process of exercising that discretion normally involves three steps:[5]

(1) The first step is to ascertain what is the property of the parties available for division. That must be calculated as at the date of the hearing, not the time of separation. Although for some purposes the fact that separation took place a long time ago may be relevant, such as the calculation of contributions made to the acquisition and preservation of property, for other purposes, such as the calculation of needs and so-called family contributions, it will be totally irrelevant that the bulk of a party's fortune was acquired after separation. From the sum-total of the assets of each of the parties there must be deducted the liabilities of each. The balance is available for distribution.

(2) The next step is to calculate the contribution each party has made to the acquisition, conservation and improvement of the property of the marriage and to the welfare of the family.[6] Essentially this relates to the period of cohabitation, including any premarital cohabitation,[7] but it can extend to the period after separation,[8] especially where there are children of the marriage to whose welfare one or both parties continue to contribute, eg by caring for them. The court may perform this assessment on an asset-by-asset basis,[9] but normally will do so globally[10] by assigning a percentage contribution figure, eg 50% to each.

(3) Finally, the court must consider the prospective needs of each party,[11] particularly those of the party (almost always the wife) in an economically weaker position with limited earning capacity and need for accommodation and child care. Since the inquiry is prospective[12] the court may under this heading consider the prospective 'financial resources' of the other

---

5   *Ferraro and Ferraro* (1992) 16 Fam LR 1 at 23; *Clauson and Clauson* (1994) 18 Fam LR 693 at 705; see Finlay, Bailey-Harris and Otlowski *Family Law in Australia*, 5th edn (Butterworths, 1997), pp 276–292.
6   Family Law Act 1975 (Cth), s 79(4)(a)–(c).
7   *Olliver and Olliver* (1978) 32 FLR 129.
8   *Ferraro and Ferraro* (1992) 16 Fam LR 1; *Gould and Gould* (1995) 20 Fam LR 1.
9   *Norbis v Norbis* (1986) 65 ALR 12; *McMahon v McMahon* (1995) 19 Fam LR 99.
10 *McLay v McLay* (1995) 20 Fam LR 239.
11 Family Law Act 1975 (Cth), s 79(4)(d)–(e).
12 See Finlay, Bailey-Harris and Otlowski op cit note 5 supra, at p 283.

party, such as future earning prospects, pension entitlements, prospective benefits under family trust arrangements and the like. Although this 'needs element' shares some of the features of spousal maintenance,[13] it is quite different in purpose.[14] A wife who may be able to support herself may still qualify for the needs factor because of a great disparity in resources. Furthermore, the needs factor looks at future capital needs, eg accommodation, rather than daily support. But the two notions tend to overlap somewhat. Under this heading the contribution figure is topped up, typically by some 10%,[15] leading to the usual common or garden variety of suburban household division of 60% to the wife and the balance to the husband.

Under s 81 of the Family Law Act 1975 (Cth) the court is instructed to make such orders as will finally resolve the financial relationships between the parties to the marriage and avoid further proceedings between them. This 'clean break' principle has been interpreted to mean that the court should avoid orders for continuing financial support for spouses, if this can be done by providing a lump sum element, either under the 'needs' factor in property division or through the provision of capitalized future support.[16]

Some of these aspects will now be discussed in greater detail.

What is 'property'?

The term 'property' is defined in s 4(1) of the Family Law Act 1975 (Cth) as 'property to which those parties are, or that party is, as the case may be, entitled, whether in possession or reversion'. The Full Court in *Duff and Duff* in 1997[17] held that it included all kinds of property both real and personal, including choses in action relying on the definition given by Langdale MR in *Jones v Skinner*[18] as descriptive of every possible interest which the party can have.

It is more useful to discuss what is *not* 'property'. Foremost is the obvious: assets not owned by either party. In Australia, like elsewhere, it is common for family businesses to be owned by private companies or family trusts. It is well established in Australian as well as in English law that the shareholders in such companies, who normally include the spouses and their children, do not own

---

13 Section 79(4)(e) of the Family Law Act 1975 (Cth) incorporates the list of factors in s 75(2) which are also relevant to an award of spousal maintenance under s 74.
14 As explained by the Full Court of the Family Court of Australia in *Clauson and Clauson* (1995) 18 Fam LR 693 at 705–706.
15 Although there is some evidence that the percentage is increasing: see the cases cited in Finlay, Bailey-Harris and Otlowski, op cit note 5 supra, 285–287; also Bailey-Harris 'The Role of Maintenance and Property Orders in Redressing Inequality: Reopening the Debate' (1998) 12 *Australian Journal of Family Law* 3 at 12–14.
16 Family Law Act 1975 (Cth), ss 74, 80(a).
17 (1977) FLC 90–217.
18 (1835) 5 LJ Ch 90.

the assets of the company. In the leading case of *Ascot Investments Pty Ltd v Harper*[19] the High Court of Australia held that the Family Law Act 1975 (Cth) did not authorise the making of orders which would defeat or prejudice the rights or nullify the powers of third parties or require them to perform duties which they were not previously liable to perform. In that case the third party was a family company which owned the husband's business but of which he was a minority shareholder, although there was some evidence to suggest that the other shareholders (his adult sons) would normally do his bidding.

However, in that case Gibbs J (as he then was) suggested that 'if a company is completely controlled by one party to a marriage, so that in reality an order against the company is an order against the party',[20] the company might fall within the powers conferred by the Act. This loophole has been exploited by the Family Court of Australia without intervention by the High Court despite several applications for leave to appeal, in cases where on the evidence it could be established that a party (almost always the husband) had followed a pattern of using the assets of the family company or trust as if they were his own through, in the case of a company, the use of a 'governing director's share' giving him all the powers of the board of directors, or in the case of a family trust by retaining the powers of an appointor or protector giving him the power to remove and replace the trustee at will and, even if not nominated as a beneficiary in the deed, having the power to nominate himself or a company in which he was a controlling shareholder, as beneficiary.[21] Thus only in the rare case of a husband having abandoned any ultimate control mechanism could it be said that the assets of the company or trust were not his.

The problem of superannuation

Another and closely related problem area is that of superannuation or pension plans. In their traditional form they were structured as trusts managed by an employer-appointed body of trustees. The employee is, in some schemes, in the position of a discretionary beneficiary with no rights to a pay-out on retirement, although the understanding is that the trustees will pay out to him or her or nominee. In most superannuation schemes which make provision for the vesting of benefits, the vesting of employer-contributed benefits and interest thereon may be subject to conditions as to period of service, quality of service and the like. In those circumstances it was not surprising that the Family Court held that superannuation, unless it had fallen due, was not 'property' but at best a contingent entitlement. Indeed some judges went so far as to compare it to an employer's gratuity upon retirement, like the proverbial gold watch, to which a wife had no entitlement even if it was paid out. However, the Full Court soon established the principle that a superannuation or pension was part of the employment package and thus should be considered

---

19 (1981) 148 CLR 337.
20 Ibid at 354–355.
21 See further Nygh and Cotter-Moroz 'The Law of Trusts in the Family Court' (1992) 6 *Australian Journal of Family Law* 4.

as part of the 'financial resources' of the beneficiary in the same manner as future earnings when it came to the consideration of the 'needs factor'.

The problem was *how* it should be considered. In the case which confirmed that superannuation was relevant to distribution, *Crapp and Crapp*,[22] the Full Court adopted what is called 'the seat of the pants approach'. It stated that some adjustment should be made out of assets existing at the time of the hearing to compensate the wife for the loss of the superannuation monies which the husband would eventually receive. The husband in that case at the time of the hearing did in fact have a vested interest in the scheme worth $A80,000 provided he then retired which was unlikely for many years. The court set aside the equal division which the trial judge had made of this sum based on a finding that contributions were equal and reduced it to $A18,000 without explaining how that figure was arrived at beyond stating that the result was 'just and equitable'. This method remains the preferred approach of the Full Court.[23]

Another method which was popular for some time was to take the notional retirement figure (the notional realisable benefit) as at the date of the hearing and divide it by a factor representing the period of cohabitation during which contributions were made. The resulting amount then in turn should be divided by the contribution factor.[24] But the Full Court frowned on this method, particularly where it resulted in the husband losing all or more than 80% of the current assets even if his earning capacity far outstripped that of the wife.[25]

An alternative method of dealing with the problem of prospective benefits was provided by legislative amendment in 1983[26] by inserting s 79(5) which allows the court to adjourn proceedings on the ground that 'there is likely to be a significant change in the financial circumstances of the parties or either of them'. This provision allows a court to make an order for the division of existing assets and then adjourn the proceedings until the superannuation falls due upon retirement. This may be a long time indeed.[27] Another variation on the same theme is to make a deferred order now which will operate on the date of retirement.[28] There are, of course, problems with this approach. In the first place, as has been pointed out, wives and children may need the money now, not at retirement.[29] Secondly, there is the problem of the premature death of

---

22 (1979) 5 Fam LR 47.
23 *Harrison and Harrison* (1996) 20 Fam LR 322.
24 *Webber and Webber* (1985) 10 Fam LR 505.
25 In *Coulter and Coulter* (1990) 13 Fam LR 421, the trial judge awarded the wife 93% of current assets; the Full Court reduced that figure to 80%, without explaining how.
26 Inserted by the Family Law Amendment Act 1983 (Cth), s 36(b).
27 In *O'Shea and O'Shea* [1998] FLC 91–964 the adjournment was for 20 years!
28 See Kay J *In the Marriage of West and Green* (1991) 16 Fam LR 811 in which the overall distribution of 50% of current assets was to be applied to superannuation benefits when they fell due in 15 years' time.
29 Millbank 'Hey Girls, have we got a Super Deal for You! Reform of Superannuation and Matrimonial Property' (1993) 7 *Australian Journal of Family Law* 104.

the superannuant.[30] The splitting of present entitlements, as is done in Germany,[31] has not been attempted as this would involve the prohibited imposition of new burdens on third parties.

Originally superannuation was the preserve of the white collar employee. It enjoyed certain tax concessions both as regards contributions and ultimate benefit. However, the previous Labor Government introduced a scheme for compulsory superannuation contributions to be made by employers under the Superannuation Guarantee Charge scheme whereby currently 6% of salary has to be paid into a recognised fund which will not be available until the employee retires after reaching the age of 55. The benefits under this scheme are vested and hence 'property', but cannot be paid out except in extraordinary circumstances with the leave of a government agency. The present Conservative coalition government has maintained the Scheme, but is unlikely to extend it as originally envisaged to a 12% contribution, including a 3% employee contribution.

The deduction of liabilities

After the assets have been added up, the liabilities must be deducted. There is little or no argument that the secured debts of the parties, such as mortgages, should be deducted. More controversial is the deduction of unsecured liabilities including unliquidated damages. In *Re Bailey*,[32] the husband was a psychiatrist who had engaged in a 'deep sleep' therapy. Some of his patients never woke up again; others were severely handicapped as a result. After he had committed suicide, his estate was faced with considerable claims exceeding $A3 million, the only property being a house worth $A250.000 which his widow sought to secure for herself. The Full Court held that

> '... it is not proper for the court to proceed in a property application without due regard to liabilities of a party which are either established or in the process of being established where the liabilities are of such magnitude as to be defeated by the order being sought in the Family Court.'[33]

The Full Court upheld the order of the trial judge granting a stay of the Family Court proceedings pending completion of the proceedings against the Bailey estate. The High Court refused to grant leave to appeal.

This decision and the policy it represents has not escaped criticism, largely on the basis that an unsecured debt ought not to be given priority over the applicant's claim because the debtor in not taking security is accepting the risk

---

30   This problem was met by Kay J *In the Marriage of West and Green* (1991) 16 Fam LR 811 by ordering the husband to take out a life policy.
31   See Chapter 3, infra. On the position in the UK, see Chapter 4, infra.
32   (1990) FLC 92–117.
33   Ibid, at 77, 774.

of the debtor's funds being depleted. *A fortiori*, contingent claims where liability has not yet been established, should not be given priority.[34] In *Hannah and Hannah*[35] Elliott J sitting at first instance had in fact preferred the wife's claim over the unsecured claims of the husband's creditors.

The Family Court has, however, acknowledged that not all debts are necessarily to be deducted. The court will refuse to deduct debts where the evidence suggests that the creditor did not really expect repayment or is seeking repayment only selectively against the applicant. Obvious examples are 'loans' made by parents of one or other of the parties which are unsecured and often undocumented, have no repayment date fixed and in respect of which interest was never demanded, even when commercial rates touched 18% in the period of high inflation. They only come alive when the marriage goes wrong and the court is often left with the reasonable suspicion that they originally were intended to be a gift to a happy couple. Another category of debt which may be disregarded is a liability incurred recklessly by one of the parties without consultation with the other and for his or her private purposes, frequently after the marriage broke down. An extreme example is the vindictive running down of the family business where after separation nothing is sold and debts are unpaid.

A related issue arises out of the bankruptcy of a spouse. It is quite clear that upon the making of the sequestration order the property ceases to be vested in the previous owner and hence is withdrawn from the property pool. In most cases that will terminate the proceedings. Although in some cases the bankruptcy is contrived (usually through the good offices of friends and relations who present dubious but uncontested claim), in most instances the debtor is truly insolvent. In such a case the solvent spouse has no claim, unless a *bona fide* settlement is reached prior to the making of the sequestration order, although the insolvent spouse may still make a claim under s 79 of the Family Law Act 1975 (Cth), albeit for the ultimate benefit of (usually his) creditors. Fortunately such examples of devotion to creditors are rare, but post-marital bitterness sometimes knows no bounds! The argument that the solvent spouse somehow has an inchoate interest in the matrimonial property has been consistently rejected. The order under s 79 adjusting the property rights of the parties creates the right of property when it takes effect and not before. Unless the applicant can rely on the creation of a resulting or constructive trust under the general law, (usually) she loses out entirely. There is no statutory right for the wife remaining in the matrimonial home even for a limited period and ejectment proceedings are likely to be taken in courts favourably inclined towards the rights of creditors.

---

34 See Lindenmayer (another member of the Appeal Division writing ex-judicially) in 'A Question of Priorities: Wives or Unsecured Creditors' (1992) 6 *Australian Journal of Family Law* 239.
35 (1989) FLC 92–052.

The assessment of contributions

In its original version, s 79[36] of the Family Law Act 1975 (Cth) directed the court to consider two types of contributions to the acquisition, maintenance and conservation of assets: financial and non-financial, including a contribution made as homemaker and parent. Some judges, however, restricted the latter to contributions made to the assets rather than the family. Hence scrubbing floors was a contribution, changing nappies does nothing to preserve the matrimonial residence! This led to the introduction of a third category in 1983:[37] the contribution made by a party to the marriage to the welfare of the family, including any contribution made as homemaker and parent. This was clearly intended to provide for the party (almost always the wife) who undertakes the home responsibilities either exclusively or after paid employment.

At first the Family Court adopted a presumption that equality should be the starting point.[38] But the High Court in *Mallet v Mallet*[39] put an end to that approach, requiring that each party's contribution be assessed in the circumstances of each case. Although the High Court stressed that the contribution of the homemaker and parent should be assessed as a substantial and not merely a token contribution, there has been a tendency to value outstanding financial contributions made by the husband far ahead of any family contribution by the wife.[40] The high point (or low point) came in the case of *Ferraro and Ferraro*[41] where the husband had amassed a fortune in property development by working long hours and leaving the children exclusively as the wife's responsibility. The trial judge, no doubt impressed by a recent visit to England where he had been on a study tour with the Family Division of the High Court, compared the husband to the builder of Sissinghurst and the wife to a mere gardener in its grounds.[42] It was the special skills and broad vision of the husband that built the family fortune. The wife merely tilled the soil and weeded the beds of the garden. The trial judge awarded her 30% of the $A10 million fortune. The Full Court in ringing tones pronouncing the inherent equality of breadwinner and homemaker upped this figure to 37.5%, feeling bound to still recognise the special 'entrepreneurial skill' of the husband's contribution. At least she did better than Lady Conran who recently received 12.5%![43]

---

36 Originally subs (3).
37 Family Law Amendment Act 1983, s 36(b), substituting a new s 79(4) into the principal Act.
38 *Wardman and Hudson* (1978) 5 Fam LR 889; see Finlay, Bailey-Harris and Otlowski *Family Law in Australia* 5th edn (Butterworths, 1997) at p 280.
39 (1984) 156 CLR 605.
40 See Finlay, Bailey-Harris and Otlowski op cit, at p 281.
41 (1993) FLC 92–335.
42 For a comment that is amusing, historical and even lyrical, see Young 'Sissinghurst, Sackville-West and Special Skill' (1997) 11 *Australian Journal of Family Law* 268; the author points out that the famous gardens were a joint project of Harold Nicholson and Vita Sackville-West.
43 *Conran v Conran* [1997] 2 FLR 615; and see the comment in [1997] Fam Law 724.

The Full Court gave a useful clarification in the subsequent case of *McLay and McLay*,[44] which concerned an estate of approximately $A9 million accumulated during the course of the marriage. Again the wife had primarily acted as home-maker and parent. The Full Court spoke of the:

> '... practical recognition of the circumstances that in many marriages each party contributes in ways which might be described as the normal way in our society and that in any qualitative evaluation of these matters the likely outcome is one of equality.'[45]

In other words, although the High Court of Australia in *Mallet* told the Family Court to investigate the details of each case and not start from a presumption of equality, it is unnecessary to bother since in almost all cases the outcome will be equality! Perhaps the Court of Appeal in England does this sometimes to the less enlightened pronouncements of the House of Lords. However, the Full Court did endorse the 'special skills' departure, but stressed that the skill lay in the application, not in the mere fact of accumulation. The outcome was 60% to the husband and 40% to the wife, the highest so far in the so-called millionaire category.

On the other hand it should be pointed out that in cases where the nett assets of the parties are smaller, as in 99% of cases, the wife with child responsibilities receives more than 50%. In such cases, despite the strictures of the High Court, there is a general judicial view in the Family Court that in a marriage of some duration in which children were born and cared for, a conclusion of equal contribution is warranted. The suggestion by some members of the High Court that every penny should be accounted for and every burnt dinner deducted is clearly not practicable. It is then common to add a 'needs component'[46] figure which normally results in an overall award of between 60% and 70%. Beyond that lies what the Full Court considers to be the irreducible minimum which the breadwinner ought to retain even if he is a high income earner but is relatively asset-poor.[47]

Another issue that has arisen in recent years is family violence. The Family Law Act 1975 (Cth) in s 75(2) lists a number of factors that are relevant to applications for spousal maintenance and property adjustment, but conduct is not one of them. The nearest factor is found in the residual paragraph (o) which refers to 'any fact or circumstances which the justice of the case requires to be taken into account'. Until recently the Full Court of the Family Court has consistently held that only factors which produce financial consequences

---

44 (1996) 20 Fam LR 239.
45 Ibid, at 250.
46 Family Law Act 1975 (Cth), s 79(4)(e).
47 As in *Coulter and Coulter* (1990) 13 Fam LR 421, where the wife had no earning capacity, had child responsibilities and the husband was earning $A85,000 per annum and had remarried and acquired a new house. He was able to borrow on the security of his superannuation entitlements. The majority of the Full Court felt that he should receive at least 20% of current assets.

should be considered.⁴⁸ This was considered to be the logical consequence of the abolition of matrimonial fault as a ground for divorce or as a disqualification for custody.⁴⁹ However, more recently, the Full Court in *Doherty and Doherty*⁵⁰ did not interfere with the trial judge's increase of the contribution figure by reference to the husband's violence on the basis that the domestic violence may well have increased the wife's contribution as a homemaker and parent. Since no reference was made to previous authority where this argument had been rejected, its authority was uncertain.⁵¹ Subsequently in *Kennon and Kennon*,⁵² the Full Court did review existing authority. It reaffirmed the conclusion in *Doherty* that domestic violence would be relevant to an assessment of contribution because it made the contribution of the victim all the more onerous.

For a time it was common to include a separate claim in tort for assault in property applications. This is possible under the cross-vesting legislation whereby the Family Court of Australia can exercise the jurisdiction of State Supreme Courts.⁵³ The practice initiated by Coleman J in *Marsh and Marsh*⁵⁴ was to entertain the common law action first, assess the damages and award the same to the victim and then assess the contribution and needs of the victim, but without taking the damages award into account. In other words the wrongdoer would have to pay the damages out of his share of the matrimonial property. The Full Court in *Kennon and Kennon*⁵⁵ threw some doubt on the utility of joining family law and common law claims, pointing out that in a common law claim each assault had to be proven separately which might create problems if violence was endemic in a long marriage. It preferred to treat violence more globally as a contribution factor under s 79(4)(c).⁵⁶ The court issued a veiled

---

48 *Fisher and Fisher* (1986) 13 Fam LR 806, where allegations that the husband had tried to drown the wife in a swimming pool were disallowed in the absence of any allegation that the attempt resulted in a reduction of her earning capacity or a need for medical treatment.
49 *Soblusky and Soblusky* (1976) 12 ALR 699.
50 (1995) 20 Fam LR 137.
51 See Behrens 'Domestic Violence and Property Adjustment: A Critique of No-Fault Discourse' (1993) 7 *Australian Journal of Family Law* 9. The author argues that violence in the home is of itself a negative contribution and therefore relevant under s 79(4)(c) of the Family Law Act 1975 (Cth).
52 (1997) 22 Fam LR 1.
53 Jurisdiction of Courts (Cross-Vesting) Acts 1987 at both Commonwealth and State levels: see Finlay, Bailey-Harris and Otlowski *Family Law in Australia* 5th edn (Butterworths, 1997), at pp 80–87. The legislation recently withstood constitutional challenge by the High Court dividing equally confirming the decision of the Full Court of the Federal Court of Australia in *BP Australia Ltd v Amann Aviation Ltd* (1996) 137 ALR 447.
54 (1993) 17 Fam LR 289.
55 Note 52 supra.
56 In making the contribution of the victim more onerous. For a comment on this approach, see Bailey-Harris 'The Role of Maintenance and Property Orders in Redressing Inequality: Reopening the Debate' (1998) 12 *Australian Journal of Family Law* 3 at 17.

threat that it might transfer future common law claims for damages for assault to the State courts as better suited to deal with them.[57]

While taking account of family violence may be salutary and just in some circumstances, it has its downside. In *Kennon* the trial of the various allegations took 10 days during which detailed allegations of various assaults were examined. Other cases to which the court referred had been marked by cross-allegations of mutual violence. Often the alleged violence was verbal rather than physical and sometimes 'symbolic', eg the husband flinging his car keys on the table instead of handing them civilly to the wife. If violence leads to an increase in shares the temptation is great to construct violence out of arguments and to enter into *tu quoque* allegations. In other words, a serious problem is easily trivialised.

MATRIMONIAL PROPERTY REFORM
The need for reform

As the foregoing discussion has shown, there are several defects in the present system. Although few judges today would consign wives to the role of tillers of the soil and weeders of the beds,[58] there is still a discernible attitude that earning large sums of money is worth more than minding the children. In general the system does not favour women: the 'clean break'[59] approach means that the wife tends to be compensated out of present assets and little or no attempt is made to compensate her for the loss of her share of the husband's future earnings. Furthermore, the discretionary system is unpredictable; some solicitors claim that they can only negotiate a settlement after they identify the judge who is to conduct the hearing, literally at the door of the court.

The situation in regard to superannuation rights is particularly unsatisfactory. The 'seat of the pants approach'[60] invariably means that the wife receives only a token amount at best. Even the financial formulae[61] employed do not take account of future benefits that the beneficiary may receive if he remains in the same employment. Empirical studies[62] have shown that the husband after separation invariably recoups his losses with superior earning and borrowing facilities intact, whereas the wife and children sink into poverty.

Another source of concern is that the present law does not permit effective pre-marital agreements. While it is possible for the parties to settle their affairs post-separation under s 87 of the Family Law Act 1975 (Cth) in a manner

---

57   Behrens and Bolas 'Violence and the Family Court: Cross-Vested Claims for Compensation' (1997) 11 *Australian Journal of Family Law* 164.
58   *Ferraro and Ferraro* (1992) 16 Fam LR 1; see also note 42 supra.
59   Family Law Act 1975 (Cth), s 81.
60   *In The Marriage of Crapp* (1979) 5 Fam LR 47.
61   See notes 24 and 25 supra.
62   Parker, Parkinson and Behrens *Australian Family in Context* (Law Book Co, 1994), chapter 12.

which, if approved by the court, will exclude further litigation,[63] this cannot be done prior to marriage. Any agreement reached is not binding upon the court, except in a historical sense. Particularly for those who enter into second marriages, some degree of certainty is desirable.

General principles of property division

In 1987 the Australian Law Reform Commission published its *Report on Matrimonial Property*.[64] Its proposals were fairly conservative and basically amounted to a codification of existing practice. The major change recommended was that a rule of equal sharing should be adopted as the starting point with a legislative reversal of the High Court's ruling in *Mallet v Mallet*.[65] It defended that proposal not only on the grounds of equity and equality but also as removing the need for raking over the minutiae of married life and avoiding value judgments about financial and household contributions.

However, the Australian Law Reform Commission recommended that the principle of equal sharing could be departed from by reference to specific considerations, for instance, the considerably greater contributions made by one party, activities of the parties after separation (both in caring for the children and negatively in not providing support), financial resources accumulated by one party during the marriage (being non-property assets such as benefits received under a discretionary trust), and gifts and inheritances, compensation received for personal injuries etc, not by way of exclusion from the divisible pool, but as a factor which might call for an adjustment in favour of the recipient. Once that process had been completed, the court would then proceed to consider any factors arising out of prospective needs and resources. As regards superannuation, the Commission recommended the application of the financial formula approach adopted by the court at that time – whereby that part of the retirement benefit as at the time of the hearing which related to the period of cohabitation – would be treated as an asset of the parties and divided on the same principle. Finally, the Commission recommended that both pre- and post-nuptial agreements be allowed and be enforceable unless they were found to have been unfair or unreasonable at the time of conclusion or the court at the time of the hearing considered that the arrangements have become unfair or unreasonable in view of subsequent events.

---

63 See Finlay, Bailey-Harris and Otlowski *Family Law in Australia*, 5th edn (Butterworths, 1997), at pp 341–344.
64 ALRC Report No 39 (AGPS, Canberra, 1987).
65 (1984) 156 CLR 605.

The proposals were never implemented even though they were endorsed by the Parliamentary Joint Select Committee in 1992.[66] In 1995 the then Labor Government introduced a Bill to reform the matrimonial property provisions in the Senate, the Family Law Reform Bill (No 2) 1995.[67] In clause 86A the Bill provided for the adjustment of property rights 'in a just and equitable way'. The guiding principle would be that the property 'be divided between the parties in proportion to their respective contributions to the marriage unless that would not produce a just and equitable result'.[68] This was backed up by a statutory assumption 'as a starting point' that they have made equal contributions, to be rebutted however if the contributions were not in fact equal.[69] The contributions to the marriage were then listed in clause 86C(2) in much the same way as in the present s 79(4), but with the starting point of equality reiterated. In addition it was made clear in clause 86C(3) that financial and non-financial contributions were to be regarded 'as being intrinsically, equally significant'.

In order to determine whether the calculations of contribution would lead to an equitable result, the court was directed in clause 86D to the 'needs factors' in much the same form as they appear in s 75(2) of the present Act. The only new provision was found in clause 86E which would have required the court to consider making the order in such a way that has the effect of retaining a business asset as a functional unit. This was inserted mainly at the urging of the farmers' lobby who were concerned at orders whereby farms had to be sold in order to give the wife a proper share of the assets. However, the clause was not intended to preserve the business in all circumstances, but only if this was practicable consistently with the court's obligations to make a division in a just and equitable way having regard to the contributions of the parties. Although the express statutory provision was new, the principle was not. Under the existing s 79(4)(d) of the Act the court must consider the impact orders will have on the earning capacity of a party, and this has been interpreted as an instruction to preserve a business if possible. Although the application of this provision cannot justify depriving a wife of her contribution entitlements, it has been invoked to cut down on the so-called 'needs factor'.[70]

---

66 Report of the Joint Select Committee on Certain Aspects of the Operation and Interpretation of the Family Law Act 1975 (AGPS, November 1992); see Finlay, Bailey-Harris and Otlowski *Family Law in Australia*, 5th edn (Butterworths, 1997), at pp 311–312.
67 See Finlay, Bailey-Harris and Otlowski op cit, at pp 312–313; Parkinson 'The Family Law Reform Bill 1 (No 2)' 10 *Australian Journal of Family Law* 1.
68 Family Law Reform Bill (No 2) 1995 (Cth), cl 86B(2).
69 Ibid, cl 86C(1).
70 Family Law Act 1975 (Cth), s 79(4)(e). In *Elsey and Elsey* (1996) 21 Fam LR 249 the trial judge awarded the wife 70%, consisting of 55% contribution and 15% to provide for her needs arising out of care of the children and the husband's superannuation entitlements. The Full Court cut this back to 60% to prevent the husband from having to sell his business, considering that such a result would be unjust to him.

These proposals were not well received. Compared to the proposals of the Australian Law Reform Commission which were fairly conservative, the 1995 Bill was a step backwards. In the Commission's proposal[71] the principle of equal sharing was the applicable rule unless one of the 'gateways' was established. In order to rebut the principle by reference to contributions a 'substantially greater contribution' had to be shown. The Bill, like the existing law, started off with a comparison of contribution, equality being only a starting point. In *McLay and McLay*[72] the Full Court appears to have moved beyond this weak presumption by declaring that special skills or other special circumstances have to be shown to avoid its preferred conclusion of equality. The declaration of the inherent equality of financial and non-financial contributions in the 1995 Bill was undoubtedly useful, but the Full Court of the Family Court of Australia had already made that declaration in *Ferraro and Ferraro*[73] and repeated it in *McLay*, supra. Even so, in neither case did the wife receive 50% of the assets. In other words, the 1995 Bill did no more than codify the law and moreover ran the risk of 'freezing' it at a point the Full Court had already passed. Fortunately, Parliament was dissolved shortly after its introduction for the General Election of 1996. Although the new government has promised to revive the Bill in a revised form, its present preoccupation with native land rights has crowded family law off the agenda. The present writer's view is that Parliament should leave this aspect well alone for the time being.

The Full Court of the Family Court of Australia appears to be lumbering towards a strong presumption that contributions are inherently equal which would be rebuttable only by special contributions or special skills. In other words, there ought to be a threshold before the presumption can be rebutted. This would mean that in 99% of cases a detailed investigation will be unnecessary. The same principle can be applied to family violence. 'Symbolic' violence should not be sufficient to cross the threshold nor occasional scuffles or abuse; only substantial acts of violence or a constant course of denigration should qualify. Furthermore the court should refrain from awarding the equivalent of punitive damages. This means that some impact must be established in the sense that the violence harmed the physical or mental health of the victim or seriously interfered with her function as homemaker and parent. Alcoholism and drug addiction, neither of which, unlike violence, are male preserves, raise similar issues. One is fearful of evidence that 'Mum had emptied the sherry before Dad came home!'; it still is a Pandora's box. Needless to say, the 1995 Bill made no reference to the impact of family violence on property division.

Where legislative intervention would be useful is in the areas of pre- and post-nuptial agreements and superannuation. In the first area legislation is required

---

71   Report No 39 Matrimonial Property, note 64 supra.
72   (1996) 20 Fam LR 239.
73   (1992) 16 Fam LR 1.

because the legal basis is presently lacking. In the latter case legislation is required because the Full Court is consistently off the right track and needs direction. Furthermore the right solution may be one which requires compliance by third parties which for constitutional reasons is at the moment beyond the power of the Family Court of Australia.

Financial agreements and pre-nuptial agreements

The Family Law Reform Bill (No 2) 1995 (Cth) made provision in respect of financial agreements and pre-nuptial agreements.[74] The former were defined[75] as agreements entered into by the parties during or after the marriage on spousal and child maintenance (the latter being subject to the Child Support legislation)[76] and property matters. Under the Bill they could be registered in a court and would thereupon operate as if they were orders of the court. Unlike the present law such agreements would not require the sanction of the court to become binding, but could be set aside if the court was satisfied that:

(1) a party's concurrence was obtained by fraud, duress or undue influence; or
(2) failure to set aside the agreement would result in serious injustice (particularly where circumstances have arisen that were not reasonably foreseeable at the time of making); or
(3) circumstances that have arisen since the agreement was entered into made it impracticable for some or all of the provisions to be carried out (in this case the court might vary the agreement instead of setting it aside); or
(4) the parties to the agreement wanted it to be set aside.[77]

Pre-nuptial agreements,[78] on the other hand, would not under the Bill require registration and their provisions would not have been enforceable as orders of the court. Their intended effect was to quarantine the property specified in the agreement with the effect that a court could not make an order under the Family Law Act 1975 (Cth) in respect of that property, although it could take its provisions into account when dealing with other property not covered by the agreement.[79] The property so quarantined could be in existence at the time of making or anticipated future property such as a likely inheritance. The requirement of specification left it unclear whether a party could quarantine all existing or future property in general terms. If not, this might have defeated the main suggested advantage of pre-nuptial agreements, namely for each party to retain present and future assets and exclude property adjustment.

---

74 Clauses 74–77D.
75 Clause 76.
76 Child Support (Assessment) Act 1989 (Cth); see Finlay, Bailey-Harris and Otlowski *Family Law in Australia*, 5th edn (Butterworths, 1997), at pp 228–260.
77 Clause 76G.
78 Defined in cl 77.
79 Clause 77D.

Under the Bill the agreement would have been variable by the parties' subsequent agreement.[80] The court was given a power to set aside or vary the agreement[81] only if:

(1) there was a property or spousal maintenance application before the court; and
(2) the court considered that it could not make an order that is just and equitable unless the agreement was set aside; and
(3) the court was satisfied that failure to set aside or vary the order would result in serious injustice.

In determining the question of serious injustice the court was to have considered various factors such as whether independent legal advice was provided before entry into the agreement, levels of understanding and literacy, and any significant change in the circumstances of the parties since entry into the agreement which were not reasonably foreseeable at the time.

Superannuation

The Family Law Reform Bill (No 2) 1975 (Cth) did not deal with superannuation, which was put in the 'too hard basket'. The present Government has promised to address the issue in its proposed legislation which because of the anticipated election this year is not likely to surface before 1999, if the issue of constitutional change which is likely to dominate that year will permit it.

The Australian Law Reform Commission in 1987[82] which was in favour of the division of the notional realisable benefit referable to the period of cohabitation as if it were an asset. In 1992 the Commission came with a new proposal in its *Report on Collective Investments: Superannuation*.[83] It suggested that the court have the power to 'split'[84] the superannuation entitlements. Instead of one account, there would be two. Thus each party would have a continuing interest in the fund and, subject to the preservation of benefits rules, have access to the fund upon reaching the age of 55 or retirement from the workforce thereafter. The division would be by court order binding directly on the entity administering the fund and not, as present, against the party who is the superannuitant, thereby giving security to the applicant spouse which is presently lacking. A somewhat similar suggestion was made in a paper prepared by the Attorney-General's Department entitled *The Treatment of Superannuation in Family Law*.[85] Like the Australian Law

---

80 Clause 77B.
81 Ibid.
82 Report No 39 *Matrimonial Property* (AGPS, Canberra, 1987).
83 ALRC Report No 59 (AGPS, Canberra, 1992), paras 12.66–12.69.
84 For recent recommendations in the UK, see *Pension Sharing on Divorce: Reforming Pensions for a Fairer Future* (DSS, June 1998).
85 Discussion Paper (AGPS, Canberra, 1992).

Reform Commission it proposed a 'split benefit' approach, but to be achieved by operation of the statute directing an equal split as at the commencement of permanent separation. Both papers suggested similar methods in which limitations on constitutional power can be overcome, and without going into details, they are persuasive.

The Joint Select Committee in its 1992 Report[86] considered both proposals and appeared to favour the latest Australian Law Reform Commission's proposal because it would maintain flexibility.[87] The Labor Government found it too difficult and the present government has not yet indicated where its sympathies lie. Of the three proposals on the table, the present writer would favour the splitting proposal which has worked in Germany for many years.[88] Moreover, an automatic rule which would avoid litigation is to be preferred, subject to the power of the court to order a departure in defined circumstances. There should also be an opportunity for the superannuitant to 'buy out' the other party's statutory entitlement with present hard cash and possibly a power in the court to order a 'buy-out' where present assets are available and there is a present need. That 'buy-out' should be on the basis of the notional realisable benefit, but with a formula not necessarily confined to the period of cohabitation since, as has been seen, there is no general rule that contribution stops at separation.

CONCLUSION

Matrimonial property law is in a constant state of flux, due to changes in social structure and relationships. When the Family Law Act 1975 (Cth) commenced operation, there may well have been a general assumption that the homemaker and parent played a lesser role. There certainly was an assumption that a 'clean break' was desirable and that, provided accommodation was supplied, the social security system would provide for the wife and children. Thus it was seen as fair to trade 60% of current assets for any further claims for support. The man went away, re-partnered and soon recouped his loss. Superannuation was only for the middle class and not appreciated as an asset; superannuation rights were generally ignored in negotiations. Family violence did not exist, or was at best confined to a drunken underclass. Because women were dependent, they had no interest in premarital agreements unless they were heiresses (rare in Australia).

All these assumptions have been falsified by subsequent events. The law has painfully lumbered towards the new realities of growing (but not yet perfected) sexual equality, the lessening role of the social security system, the increasing importance of superannuation as an asset and the discovery of family violence as a general problem. One possible response is to leave it to the

86   See note 66 supra.
87   Ibid, paras 9.58–9.61.
88   See Chapter 3.

judges to respond to these new realities and adjust the law accordingly. In some respects the response of the Full Court has been much better than the various proposals for reform where the risk of 'freezing' the law is great. But there are other areas such as premarital agreements and superannuation where legislation is necessary and the development of the law cannot be left to judges. Furthermore, the 'clean break' principle, although re-asserted in the 1995 Bill, should be reconsidered. Future inequalities in income and resources can only be remedied by spousal maintenance.[89]

---

89 See Bailey-Harris 'The Role of Maintenance and Property Orders in Redressing Inequality: Reopening the Debate' (1998) 12 *Australian Journal of Family Law* 3.

Chapter 3

DIVIDING THE ASSETS ON FAMILY BREAKDOWN: THE GERMAN CIVIL CODE[1]

Professor Horst Lücke[2]

INTRODUCTION

Family breakdown may or may not be followed by divorce. In either situation, there may be a division of the family assets. In Germany, as in many other countries,[3] the property relations of married couples, including the problems of division on breakdown, are governed by the rules of a matrimonial property regime, either the regime chosen by the spouses or, if no choice was made, the one applicable by operation of law. These regimes never apply to unmarried relationships. When they break up, other rules may have to be applied to bring about the division of the parties' assets. It might be the rules on unjust enrichment, on joint ownership of property or, most importantly, on civil law partnerships.

In German law the rules about the division of the assets of married couples are activated by the termination of matrimonial property regimes. There is no general principle mandating a division of property when a family breakdown occurs without divorce. Divorce, however, brings property regimes to an end and for this reason triggers the division of property.

In contrast to common law countries, Germany has a long matrimonial property tradition. Until well into the 19th century the country's matrimonial property law was completely fragmented. Before the introduction of the Civil

---

1 The following abbreviations have been used:
   BGH   Bundesgerichtshof (Federal Supreme Court of Justice)
   BGHZ   Entscheidungen des Bundesgerichtshofs in Zivilsachen (Decisions of the Federal Supreme Court of Justice in Civil Matters)
   BVerfG   Bundesverfassungsgericht (Federal Constitutional Court)
   BVerfGE   Entscheidungen des Bundesverfassungsgerichts (Decisions of the Federal Constitutional Court)
   FamRZ   Familienrechtszeitschrift (Family Law Journal)
   IECL   International Encyclopedia of Comparative Law
   JR   Juristische Rundschau (Legal Review)
   JZ   Juristenzeitung (Legal Review)
   NJW   Neue Juristische Wochenschrift (New Legal Weekly Journal)
   OLG   Oberlandesgericht (Higher Regional Court)
2 Professor Emeritus (Adelaide), Research Associate (Max-Planck-Institute, Hamburg).
3 See the comparative survey in Rheinstein and Glendon, *International Encyclopedia of Comparative Law* (IECL) IV ch 4, 4–34 et seq.

Code in 1900, almost any conceivable type of system could be found somewhere in Germany.[4] From this patchwork the draftsmen of the Civil Code developed five prototypes:

(1) administration and usufruct (whereby the husband administered the wife's property and was entitled to the income from it);
(2) separation of goods;
(3) community of goods;
(4) community of earnings;
(5) community of movable goods.

The Code gave marriage partners the right to choose under which of these regimes they wanted to live. When they failed to make a choice, the 'legal' regime (administration and usufruct) applied.

Post-war German legal developments in matrimonial property law have been influenced decisively by the constitutional affirmation of the value of marriage and the family (Art 6 I of the Basic Law)[5] on the one hand, and by the idea of equality of men and women (Art 3 II of the Basic Law)[6] on the other. The Basic Law gave the Government some time to bring the law into harmony with the equality principle. Art 117 I reads: 'Legislation which is inconsistent with Art 3 II shall remain in force until adapted to that provision of the Basic Law but not beyond 31 March 1953.' The Government failed to adapt German family law (the fourth book of the German Civil Code) by the crucial date, and large parts of it became ineffective. This exposed the country to a four-year transition period, during which much of the law of the old regimes had been swept away by the Constitution and no new law had taken its place. In the absence of choice, the regime which governed marriages then was that of separation of goods. The transition period came to an end in 1957 when the Equality Act amended the Code and introduced three systems:

(1) the community of accrued gains[7] ('Zugewinngemeinschaft') (§§ 1363–1390);
(2) the separation of goods (§ 1414); and
(3) the community of property (§§ 1415–1518).

The Constitutional Court has the power of judicial review and will see to it that every legislative provision is consistent with the Constitution. In family law, Art 6 I and Art 3 II and III of the Basic Law are especially important. German constitutional theory recognises that two provisions of the Basic Law

---

4   Rheinstein and Glendon, IECL IV ch 4, 4–48 et seq.
5   'Marriage and family enjoy the special protection of the state.'
6   'Men and women have equal rights'; Art 3 III adds: 'Nobody shall be prejudiced or favoured because of their sex ...' The article also mentions birth, race, language, national or social origin, faith, religion and political opinion as factors which must not lead to prejudicial or favoured treatment.
7   This is the translation suggested by Goren (transl) *The German Civil Code* (Rothman & Co, Littleton, Col 1994).

might have to be reconciled and, in the process, qualify each other. If 'marriage' means 'Christian marriage' and if that implies certain forms of inequality, can that override Art 3? Is the 'housewife marriage' (a single-income marriage in which only the husband works and attracts an income) part of the concept of the Christian marriage? Is the splitting of income for tax purposes (which carries tax advantages for the traditional housewife marriage) unconstitutional? There are many problems for the Constitutional Court, which could not arise in a system like that of the United Kingdom. It is with this background in mind that one must seek to give an account of the problems of dividing property in cases of family breakdown.

This is not the place for a detailed analysis of the constitutional significance of the equality principle. It has led to decisions of the courts, including the Constitutional Court, concerning such questions as: Can a man be disqualified by law from becoming a midwife? Is the Civil Code free to allow only women to sue for breach of promise (sexual intercourse having been permitted in expectation of marriage)? Which family name is the proper name for the family and the children?

I. FAMILY BREAKDOWN: DIVISION OF PROPERTY UNDER MATRIMONIAL PROPERTY REGIMES

Because of their great importance to the daily life of the parties, the matrimonial home and its contents (furnishings, household equipment) have been subjected to a special regime. The organisation of separate households has usually taken place even before a divorce is pronounced, for one of the most frequent forms of divorce is the divorce based upon a separation which has lasted one year or more, and the need for separate accommodation will usually have existed for the whole of that period. §§ 1361a and 1361b of the Civil Code, which apply to all cases of separation, deal with this question. The measures which a court may take under these rules are of a provisional nature only, and are not available to parties who have decided upon a permanent separation without divorce, perhaps because their religion prohibits divorce.

§ 1361a is concerned with the contents of the matrimonial home. It states that each spouse is entitled to his or her own property, but adds immediately that, within the limits of fairness, spouses are obliged to allow each other to keep those items which are needed for the conduct of a separate household. What fairness requires depends on all the circumstances, including the needs and interests of children if any.

The matrimonial home is dealt with in a similar way in § 1361b. The ownership of the home is an especially important circumstance. Yielding the whole or part of a home which one owns to the other spouse may be required only when that is necessary to prevent severe hardship, and then only against payment of compensation, if that would be equitable.

The Family Court has jurisdiction to make orders giving effect to the principles which govern home and contents, but such orders lose their effect upon divorce when the final distribution is determined by the Family Court. When these problems arise in that context, German courts are not guided by the Civil Code, but by the Regulations on the treatment of the matrimonial home and its contents of 21 October 1944, a measure which was prompted by the severe housing shortage during the latter stages of World War II. Under these Regulations, which have been amended and are still in force today, the Family Court may make orders in relation to home and contents only if the parties are unable to come to an amicable agreement about all the matters which need to be settled. § 1 reads:

> 'If in the context of the divorce, the spouses cannot agree which of them should in future occupy the matrimonial home and which party should receive the furnishings and domestic equipment, the judge will make orders concerning the legal relations which govern these matters.'

It is settled that, to the extent that the Family Court has power to distribute these assets, they are not subject to the matrimonial property regime applicable to the spouses' property relations. Existing rights are not necessarily binding upon the judge, but he must take them into account. In the case of the contents, the judge will use his discretion, but must be guided by considerations of fairness and equity (§ 2). In the case of the dwelling, property rights will weigh more heavily in the balance. If both spouses are co-owners, the same principle prevails as in the case of contents. If, however, the dwelling is the property of one of the spouses, the judge is able to assign it to the other only if this is necessary to avoid unacceptable hardship (§ 3).

The powers wielded by the Family Court under these Regulations are considerable. If parties have rented their matrimonial home, the judge dealing with the divorce has the power to dictate to the landlord a new tenancy agreement to give effect to what seems to him a sensible arrangement for the parties (§ 5).

1. The separation of goods and the community of property regime

The separation of goods was the normal regime during the transition period from 1953–1957. It was then much criticised as being incompatible with the marriage relationship. It is now considered quite suitable in cases in which both parties own a good deal of property and do not want to leave things to chance. If the parties are divorced, the division of the property raises no special problems in theory, for each has retained his and her own assets throughout the marriage. Nevertheless, problems often do arise, for the closeness of their union may have given rise to problems of delimitation. One may have contributed financially to an expensive house, which is, for some reason, registered in the name of the other. In common law jurisdictions, the trust would be employed to resolve such situations. In German law, the courts resort to the device of an implied civil law partnership or association (§ 705–740 of the Civil Code), which requires liquidation and a proper distribution of the assets including any gains which might have been made.

The community of property regime can only come into existence by matrimonial contract. Much of the property owned by the spouses when this regime commences becomes common property. Divorce brings the regime to an end and thereafter the common property has to be divided. The division does not necessarily occur in equal parts. In the divorce court each of the parties may request that the common property be divided so as to restore to each what he or she has brought into the marriage (§ 1478). This regime is rarely agreed upon these days and will not be dealt with further in this study.

2. The community of accrued gains

This regime comes into effect by operation of law when the parties have not chosen one of the others. It governs the overwhelming majority of marriages. The German phrase is also translated as 'community of acquests'[8] or 'community of surplus'.[9] The parties retain their separate properties (§ 1363 II)[10] and each administers his or her property independently (§ 1364). Even things acquired during the marriage become the property of the spouse who acquires them. As in the separation of goods regime, there is no common fund owned jointly by both parties at any stage, whether before, during or after the marriage. The description of the regime as a 'community' is, at least in a property sense, a misnomer. German writers suggest that the regime should be called 'separation of goods with equalisation of accrued gains'.[11]

When the regime ends, the community of accrued gains manifests itself only in the form of an obligation for money to be paid (§ 1378).[12] The assets acquired by the parties during their marriage are 'equalised', ie their respective values are ascertained and added together, and the party with the lesser increase is given a right to claim the amount of money needed to give both equal shares.[13] The imposition of an obligation to hand over actual items of property is very much the exception. It never arises by operation of law, but only by judicial *fiat*. The Family Court has the power to make such orders on the twofold precondition that this would prevent gross unfairness to the claimant and that it would not be unreasonable from the point of view of the other party (§ 1383). The power

---

8   Rheinstein and Glendon, IECL IV ch 4, 4–79.
9   Cohn, *Manual of German Law* 2nd edn (Oceana Publications, Inc, 1968) I, 237.
10 'The property of the husband and the property of the wife will not become joint property of the spouses; this also applies to property acquired by a spouse after entering the marriage.'
11 Beitzke, *Familienrecht, Ein Studienbuch* 25th edn (CH Beck, München, 1988) 107.
12 'If the accrued gains of one exceed those of the other spouse, then that other has an equalisation claim amounting to half the difference.... This claim arises at the termination of the regime and is inheritable and assignable thereafter.'
13 'Gains made by the spouses during the marriage will be equalised if the community of accrued gains comes to an end.' (§ 1363 II).

is rarely used, so there is very little case-law. An obvious example would be a valuable heirloom from the family of the claimant which happens to be the property of the other party.

The regime does not necessarily come into being the moment the parties marry. They may have agreed on one of the other regimes but during their marriage may make a further matrimonial contract adopting the community of accrued gains (§ 1408 I). The Federal Supreme Court of Justice has held that they may even do so with retrospective effect to the time of conclusion of their marriage if they have lived in the separation of goods regime (BGH NJW 94, 343).

a. Termination of the regime

One must inquire into the circumstances which bring the regime to an end, for § 1378 III states: 'The equalisation claim arises upon the termination of the regime and is inheritable and assignable thereafter.' The regime may end even when there is no breakdown of the marriage, for the parties may simply agree to end it because it no longer suits them. This brings about the separation of goods (unless they agree to adopt the community of goods), as does an agreement which is confined to the exclusion of the equalisation claim (which is the essence of the community of accrued gains regime) (§ 1414).[14] Such an agreement gives rise to an equalisation claim but may not involve any kind of crisis. Probably the most important event causing the termination of the regime is still death. Should the spouses die at the same time (there is no *commorientes* presumption), the regime obviously comes to an end, but there is no equalisation of gains. The death of one of the parties does not always lead to an equalisation of the gains made during the marriage. Instead, § 1371 I decrees that the surviving spouse's share of the deceased estate is increased by one quarter of the estate.[15]

In Germany, as elsewhere, many marriages end in divorce, and once a divorce judgment (§ 1564) becomes final, the regime comes to an end and an equalisation claim arises. Other grounds are the annulment of a marriage (Marriage Law § 28, 29) and the declaration of nullity of an invalid marriage (Marriage Law § 23). The regime may also come to an end because one of the parties has obtained a judgment ordering its premature termination.

If a couple lives separately for three years, either party may claim premature equalisation of the accrued gains (§ 1385). This does not involve an automatic termination; it merely makes it possible for either party to bring it to an end by court action. Proceeding with such a claim even if a divorce is not, or at least is not immediately, envisaged, may be in the interest of both parties. The party who has had fewer gains can perhaps look forward to a substantial financial boost; the other will be interested in closing the books and making sure that he

---

14 If parties to the regime of community of goods agree to end it, the same result follows: separation of goods is the consequence (§ 1414).
15 Equalisation in such a case takes place if the surviving spouse has been disinherited.

or she need not share any future gains. When a judgment awarding premature equalisation becomes final, the community of accrued gains is terminated and is replaced by the separation of goods regime (§ 1388). One might wonder why a serious separation of the parties does not trigger an equalisation claim immediately, for, in a sense, the basis for further sharing disappears as soon as the parties separate. It seems that the Code considers that a three-year waiting period is a safeguard against separations which are simply motivated by the desire to share in the gains of the other side.

b. The equalisation calculation

The Code defines 'accrued gains' as 'the amount by which the final assets (existing at the termination of the regime) of a spouse exceed his or her initial assets (existing at the commencement of the regime)' (§ 1373). The key concepts in the equalisation calculation are 'initial assets' and 'final assets'. For each party, the value of the accrued gains is ascertained by valuing the final assets (which include the initial assets), and then deducting the value of the initial assets. If the value of the accrued gains of one spouse exceeds that of the other, the excess is then divided by two and the spouse who has gained less may claim half the difference from the other.

The purpose of this determination is not the identification of various premarital and post-marital aggregates of property (*Vermögensmassen*). Initial assets and final assets are simply the figures in an arithmetic calculation intended to establish how much money should be paid in order to achieve, in monetary terms, an equalisation of the accrued gains. The Code has chosen this path because it has eliminated the complex task of tracing items of property to establish to which fund they belong.

It is very much in keeping with this thinking that real increases in the value of particular premarital assets during the marriage (eg shares which increase in value), as distinct from nominal increases due to inflation, are considered to be accrued gains. Admittedly, this is viewed critically in the literature.[16] The Code has given the courts very little guidance concerning the impact of inflation, but the Federal Supreme Court of Justice has held that the valuation of the initial assets should take the factor of inflation into account, using the Consumer Price Index (CPI) as the relevant guide (BGHZ 61, 385). It must be doubtful whether this is a really useful indicator of the true value of items other than the consumables used to establish the CPI. However, a better indicator is not available.

Inflation raises odd questions, although Germany has not seen rampant inflation for many years. Assume that a spouse had a debt of DM 100 000 before the marriage. That would have to be deducted from his or her assets at

---

16 Battes, *Ehegewinn und eheneutraler Erwerb – Eine Grundsatzfrage des gesetzlichen Güterrechts*: Bosch (ed), *Neuere Entwicklungen im Familienrecht* (Schriften zum Bürgerlichen Recht Band 122) (Berlin, Duncker & Humblot, 1990) 49, 62. The Austrian solution is to exclude such increases from the equalisation.

the time of the marriage. Assume further that the debt is paid five years later when the value of money has fallen by 50%. A majority of writers take the view that the spouse has made a gain of DM 50 000, which is subject to equalisation.[17]

'Final assets' and 'initial assets' are very far from being purely factual concepts. Considerations of fairness and of other policy aims play decisive roles in a variety of departures from the actual facts. Many of the rules which make up the regime are concerned with the determination of the two sets of assets.

i. The final assets

To determine the final assets of a spouse, any liabilities existing at the relevant time are deducted from the value of the actual assets, but only to the extent of the value of the assets (§ 1375 I).[18] The Code does not work with a concept of negative assets. If it were otherwise, the party with gains would have to share those, not only to the extent that they exceed any gains of the other, but also to the extent of helping the other wipe out his or her debts. The Code obviously did not want to create a duty to use one's own gains to help the other avoid bankruptcy. There is an aversion to the incurring of debts which are not covered by one's assets.

If, within the 10 years preceding the termination of the regime, a spouse has diminished his or her assets in order to disadvantage the other spouse, or has wasted assets or indulged in gratuitous dispositions for which there was no sufficient (moral or other) basis, any assets so lost are notionally added to his or her actual assets again (§ 1375 II).

In many marriages, it is not only when the marriage is dissolved that sharing takes place. If H has won a large amount of money in a lottery (say DM 100 000), he might give half of it to W. Is this to be ignored when it comes to a parting of the ways? If H were a lawyer, he might say to W: 'Should our accrued gains ever have to be equalised, this money is to be considered an advance equalisation.' H's prudent comment will have brought his gift under § 1380 I, sent 1.[19] The provision would be unrealistic if it were not for the next sentence which introduces an important presumption: 'In case of doubt it is to be presumed that such transactions are to be taken into account if their value exceeds that of occasional gifts which would be considered normal given the circumstances of the particular couple.' § 1380 II requires that the value of the gift be notionally added to the final assets of the donor before it is deducted

---

17 Staudinger, *Kommentar zum Bürgerlichen Gesetzbuch* 13th edn (Berlin, Sellier-de Gruiter, 1994) § 1373 n 19. The Federal Supreme Court of Justice has come to the opposite conclusion – BGHZ 109, 89, 95.
18 There is one exception; see §§ 1375 I, 1390.
19 'The value of things received by a spouse through a legal transaction *inter vivos* from the other with the proviso that it should be taken into account in any equalisation, are to be deducted from the equalisation claim.' If H were an academic lawyer, he might add: 'By the way, should your accrued gains be greater than mine, you will not have to pay part of this back, for as a donation, it will fall under § 1374 II' (supra).

from the equalisation claim. For both purposes, the value is to be ascertained as at the time of the donation. It seems that it is only ever the equalisation debtor who can benefit from these provisions. If the creditor (ie the party who has gained less) has made a large donation, he or she will receive no kind of compensation for it. This occasional unfairness may be the hallmark of a system which applies a simple formula instead of making the result depend on all the circumstances of particular cases.

ii. The initial assets
The value of the initial assets represents the figure to be deducted from the value of the final assets so as to determine how much is relevant for the final reckoning. The value of the initial assets will be excluded. It will be treated as irrelevant to the equalisation. Generally speaking, these are the assets which a party has brought into the marriage.

Bequests and gifts acquired by a spouse after the conclusion of the marriage are to be notionally included in the initial assets (§ 1374 II). It follows that these are accrued gains which are not to be subjected to equalisation. The most plausible rationale of this provision is that such items are rather personal and that the donor in such cases would not have wished such property to benefit the other party to the divorce. Damages for pain and suffering for the tort of a third party during the marriage are also rather personal but are nevertheless to be included in the final assets.

As in the case of the final assets, liabilities must be excluded in working out the value of the initial assets, but only to the point where the assets are nil (§ 1374 I). Again, there is no concept of negative assets. If it were used, the result is best illustrated by an example. If W uses her income to help H during the marriage over a premarital debt of say DM 100 000 and the marriage fails, W might wish to claim her share of this benefit (DM 50 000). Her claim will not succeed.

When describing the 50/50 formula as simple, one should not forget that its application may be very difficult. When a marriage has lasted for many years, it will not be easy for the parties to work out the initial and the final assets. The Code has introduced presumptions to help overcome some of the difficulty. According to § 1377, if the parties establish an inventory of their respective assets, its contents will be presumed to be correct; if they fail to do so, it will be presumed that the final assets also represent the accrued gains. Each spouse has a right to the cooperation of the other in drawing up such an inventory. The presumptions are rebuttable, but they must be of great assistance to the courts when, after many years of marriage, evidence is truly hard to find. § 1377 is hardly compatible with a romantic concept of marriage,[20] but in this respect it is no different from most other matrimonial property rules.

---

20   Cohn has been rather scathing about these arrangements (op cit 238).

The time relevant for the valuation of the initial assets is the time at which the regime commences. This is usually the day on which the parties are married. The parties might agree when they marry to use another regime and then later choose the regime of community of accrued gains instead. That will then be the relevant time. A somewhat controversial question arises when parties determine by marriage contract that the time of commencement for the regime is to be backdated to a particular date in the past. This would be appropriate in the fairly common case of the trial marriage followed by an actual wedding. The majority view (*herrschende Meinung*) is that this is permissible, but there is a respectable view to the contrary.

c. Protection of the equalisation claim

As is apparent from some of the provisions relevant to the determination of the value of assets, the Code seeks by various means to protect the equalisation claim from being diminished by manipulation and other detrimental conduct. § 1375 II, which deals with wastefulness, intentional diminution and inappropriate generosity towards third parties (supra) is clearly designed to serve this purpose. Many other provisions have been included with this aim in mind.

i. Restraints on alienation

Further measures pointing in the same direction are certain limits being placed on the parties' power of alienation during the marriage, not only to preserve the existing basis of their relationship, but also their future rights. A spouse may undertake to dispose of his or her assets as a whole only with the consent of the other (§ 1365). The courts have extended this limitation also to situations which involve the alienation of things which represent the bulk of the property owned by a spouse (BGHZ 77, 293). Such a transaction is thought to be a threat to the rights of the other because the liquidation of assets is often a first step towards concealment or placing them out of the reach of legal action. Things which are part of the parties' domestic establishment (*Haushaltsgegenstände*) are also given some legal protection. When they are replaced, the replacement items belong to the party who owned the original item (§ 1370). Moreover, the owner of such an item is not allowed to undertake to sell it or to alienate it without the consent of the other (§ 1369). Perhaps the main purpose of these provisions is to preserve the basis of the parties' joint living from unilateral sabotage by one or the other, but the preservation of the potential claim to equalisation is obviously a further aim.[21]

ii. Further cases of premature termination

The desire to protect the equalisation claim is also apparent from the provisions concerning the premature termination of the regime (ie a

---

21 In their review of the world's matrimonial property systems, Rheinstein and Glendon are inclined to deny the community of accrued gains the right to be described as a 'matrimonial property system'. This criticism seems misplaced, for there are quite genuine changes in the parties' property relations which justify calling the system a matrimonial property regime.

termination taking place before the marriage is dissolved) (§ 1385). This may or may not involve the breakdown of the marriage.

According to § 1386, premature equalisation may be demanded in the event of certain objectionable conduct. The emphasis is not on old-style matrimonial offences like adultery or desertion, but on conduct with negative economic and financial implications. Four situations are envisaged:

(1) One of the spouses culpably defaults in the fulfilment of his or her economic matrimonial obligations for an extended period and there is good reason to think that this will continue. Possible instances are the persistent failure of the working spouse to make his or her contribution to the upkeep of the household or the failure of the non-working spouse to look after the household in the appropriate way. If the spouse who has gained more during the marriage happens to be the victim of such treatment, premature termination of the regime and equalisation will be of no immediate use to him or her.

The other three situations involve conduct which places a future equalisation claim in jeopardy. They are as follows: a spouse has

(2) concluded a transaction contrary to § 1365 (supra);
(3) decreased his or her assets contrary to § 1375 (supra);
(4) has persistently refused without sufficient justification to supply information about his or her assets.

It appears that these cases and the three-year separation are intended by the Code as conclusive. It follows that other circumstances such as bankruptcy, the cultivation of a gambling habit or the appointment of a guardian will not give rise to a premature equalisation claim.

iii. The time factor in the determination of the final assets
The relevant time for the determination of the final assets is usually the time at which the property regime ends. An exception to this rule is made in the case of divorce, when the relevant time for calculating the value of the final assets is not the termination of the regime (which occurs when the divorce takes effect), but the filing of the divorce petition (§ 1384), so as to make manipulation during the final phase of the marriage more difficult.

In the case of a claim for premature equalisation, the value of the final assets is determined as at the time of the filing of the claim. As in the case of divorce, the Code considers that during the proceedings the risk of manipulation is particularly acute.

d. Hardship and unfairness
'Accrued gains', like all legal concepts, has some fuzzy edges. Is the paying-off of a premarital liability such a gain? Reverting to the case of a wife who, during the marriage, has helped her husband over a premarital debt of DM 100 000, let us assume that W has, in addition, saved DM 100 000. If the basic approach is applied, H would be able to claim DM 50 000 as equalisation. The Code is

not indifferent to such hardship. § 1381 I allows the equalisation to be resisted if it would be grossly inequitable. An example given is the case of a spouse who during an extended period defaulted culpably in the fulfilment of his or her economic matrimonial obligations (§ 1381 II). As one would expect, there is a good deal of case-law which has amplified this provision. The courts will only apply it in cases in which granting equalisation would shock the conscience. A court would not accept the argument that an asset should be excluded merely because the other spouse had not contributed to its acquisition.[22] The equalisation provisions are a standard solution for the vast majority of cases, creating predictability and certainty and enabling parties to work out their legal rights without resort to litigation. It is not the function of § 1381 to allow every case to be decided according to its particular merits.

The equalisation claim may involve large amounts of money. Assume that H has built up a valuable business as a married man and now faces divorce. The Family Court has the power to impose a moratorium on an equalisation obligation 'if immediate payment would be inappropriate, bearing in mind also the interests of the party entitled to equalisation' (§ 1382). Relevant situations are that such payment would pose a threat to the business conducted by the equalisation debtor, that he or she would be forced to sell items of property at give-away prices, or that it would prejudice the living conditions of joint children. The court could use this power to save H's business. If a moratorium is ordered, the debtor will be obliged to pay such interest and to provide such security as the court may determine.

II. FAMILY BREAKDOWN: ADJUSTMENT OF PENSION ENTITLEMENTS

1. Pensions: a complex and vitally important part of the 'social net'

Nowhere are pension entitlements more important than in Germany. There is an army of public servants and their old age and invalidity are secured by non-contributory public service pension entitlements (*Rentenanwartschaften*). For the rest of the workforce, substantial levies on employers and employees to provide insurance against unemployment and invalidity and income maintenance in old age are a compulsory part of most employment contracts (jobs which pay no more than DM 610 a month are excluded) and the benefits provided tend to be generous. One expects to live on them fairly comfortably during one's retirement or in the event of invalidity. Employees and workers have their pension entitlements under the 'contract between the generations' which are administered by federal and state authorities. The mining industry has its own system for its employees, also run by a state agency. Farmers have

---

22 This might be explained by stressing that even things acquired only by the efforts of one spouse accrue to both because they were not used for consumption when they could have been. Battes op cit.

their own statutory pension scheme. Professional groups like doctors or lawyers have pension arrangements. There are private pension arrangements of various types, not assisted by the state. Many though not all pensions administered by state agencies are 'dynamic' (*dynamisiert*), ie they are adjusted in accordance with changes in the average earnings of the workforce. Pensions payable under private pension schemes tend not to share in this quality and lack the state subsidies needed to finance such a system.

This complicated system of pensions (together with the system of social welfare payments, although they are not relevant in our present context) represents what is often referred to as the 'social net'. Germany's economic problems have made the outlook rather gloomy, but many people still rely entirely on the comfort of the net. Germans would hardly be world champions in foreign travel if they had to put money aside themselves for these purposes. The pension entitlement is often the most valuable asset they possess and its legal treatment a matter of the utmost importance. Amendments to the Civil Code in 1970 introduced pension adjustment (often by way of pension splitting) as one of the consequences of divorce and this system has existed now for nearly 30 years. In view of the discussions taking place in Britain, it might be of interest to explore the options from which the German legislator was able to choose when this system was being prepared.

2. Pensions: legislative options

a. Pensions and maintenance after divorce

Pensions are concerned with maintenance and one might consider that pensions after divorce should simply be subsumed under the ordinary maintenance rules. In Germany the rule is that a divorced person who is not able to provide for his or her own maintenance may claim maintenance from the former spouse (§ 1569). Such a claim is triggered solely by the needs of one of the parties and the ability of the other to pay. The divorce law itself is no longer concerned with matrimonial offences, with guilt or innocence in causing the marriage breakdown. It follows that such factors should also be irrelevant for the determination of maintenance obligations after divorce. The legal basis for a maintenance obligation, designed to last a lifetime even after divorce, is, as Beitzke explains, 'the mutually undertaken responsibility of the spouses for each other's welfare, which, in view of the lifelong bond created by marriage, is not brought to an end by divorce'.[23] A maintenance obligation is excluded if it would be grossly inequitable (*groß unbillig*) to impose it (§ 1579). Maintenance obligations come to an end with the death of the creditor (§ 1586). The same applies when the creditor remarries, but even then a limited possibility of revival of the earlier claim exists if the second marriage fails (§ 1586a). The death of the debtor does not extinguish the obligation which remains as a liability of the deceased estate (§ 1586b). This system may seem inappropriate

---

23   Op cit 171 et seq.

to some, but the German Constitutional Court has declared it to be consistent with the Constitution (BVerfG NJW 1981, 1771).

Solving the problem of sharing pensions by relying on the maintenance rules would mean that, having collected his or her pension, the maintenance debtor would be expected to pay over the appropriate part of it to the former spouse. Such an obligation would have practical consequences when the maintenance debtor becomes an old-age pensioner, which time usually coincides with the cessation of work and a substantial drop in income. To insist that, at such a time, the kind of compulsory solidarity demanded by the German system should be continued on a much more difficult basis, is not likely to yield very satisfactory results. The difficulty might be counteracted to some extent by legislating to give the relevant pension fund authority to make direct payment of the appropriate share of the pension to the maintenance creditor. However, the maintenance creditor would remain dependent upon the debtor in other ways. None of the fringe benefits (like insurance for medical expenses), associated with state pensions particularly, would benefit the maintenance creditor and this source of maintenance would cease to exist with the death of the debtor.[24] This would cause problems in many (former) housewife marriages, for the ex-husband (usually the maintenance debtor) often predeceases his ex-wife.

b. Pensions and matrimonial property regimes

It has been said that entitlements against our modern welfare state are a new form of property.[25] The German Constitutional Court has recognised that even the pensions available under compulsory state pension schemes are property within the meaning of Art 14 of the Basic Law (the constitutional guarantee which declares unconstitutional the taking of property by the state without compensation). This characterisation of pensions suggests that they be dealt with as part of the matrimonial property regime which happens to govern the parties' property relations. In one respect (and in one respect only) the reaction of the German legislator to such an approach was very positive. The basic principle that gains accrued during a marriage be shared equally after its breakdown, which is the essence of the community of accrued gains regime (supra), must have seemed very attractive, for it was in fact extended to pensions.

The Civil Code has a segment, inserted in 1970, under the heading 'Equalisation of Value of Expectations or Promises of a Pension'. This reform was introduced in order to improve the situation of women who had been caught in an unsatisfactory housewife marriage. In testimony before the Constitutional Court in 1980, the Ministry of Justice explained that, before the

---

24 This consequence might be avoided by a widow's pension, available under some pension schemes to divorced wives.
25 Reich, C, 'The New Property': 73 *Yale Law Journal* 733 at 738–739 (1964); Glendon *The Transformation of Family Law* (Chicago and London, 1989) 135.

reforms, the position of many women had been gravely prejudiced by the law, and that the reforms had improved this by severing the old-age provision for women from the whole concept of maintenance and in giving them independent support. The Ministry considered that the reforms had been justified by the partnership relationship which had existed between the ex-spouses; their contributions had to be regarded as equal, even though they might have resulted in very different pension entitlements.

The programme of adjustment is announced in § 1587: 'A pension adjustment takes place between divorced spouses if, during the period of their marriage, entitlements to or expectancies of old-age, invalidity or disability pensions of the type specified in § 1587a II[26] were created or maintained.' The basic adjustment principle is stated in (§ 1587a I): 'The spouse liable to such an adjustment is the one who has the more valuable entitlement or expectancy. The other spouse has a right to an adjustment to the extent of half the difference between the respective values.'[27] This seemingly simple approach is very similar to that which governs the community of accrued gains: during their marriage the parties have worked together to produce or maintain such an entitlement; the nature of their union was such that they should have enjoyed the fruits of it later in life together; if so, it seems only fair that they should now, when things have turned out differently, benefit equally from it, though only to the extent that it was acquired while they were married.

This basis for the adjustment of pensions is consistent with the exclusion of those pension entitlements (like the Australian old-age pension) which have resulted neither from the performance of work nor from the employment of capital on the part of the spouses (§ 1587 I, sent 2). Apart from this limitation, the system of pension adjustment is intended to be comprehensive. It applies not just to a limited number but to all pensions. This raises questions of delimitation, for property and pension income have to be distinguished. Not everything which produces an income at regular intervals is a pension. Bank accounts which yield interest periodically or shares which yield dividends are not included. Life insurance which yields a capital payment at age 65 is not included, but if it yields a pension entitlement at a specified age it will be included. If it yields a right to opt for one or the other, the courts will ask whether the right to opt had been exercised prior to the filing of the divorce petition (BGHZ 88, 386). These problems of fine-tuning need not be pursued further; their comparative interest is limited by the fact that pension entitlements in Britain will not be entirely comparable with their German counterparts.

---

26 § 1587a II, a many-faceted and most elaborate provision, is concerned with the actual valuation of such entitlements.
27 This scheme seems to be rather similar to the scheme envisaged for England and Wales under the amended version of the Matrimonial Causes Act 1973, s 25B(2)(c).

Pension adjustment is based upon much the same thinking as that which has inspired the community of accrued gains. From this has followed an important limitation. It is not the full pension entitlement which is to be adjusted, but only such part of it as has accrued during the marriage. This seems justified by the thought that it is the parties' joint life and work which has resulted in the pension entitlement and that has, generally speaking, taken place during matrimony. The Code specifies the relevant period as commencing with the first day of the month in which the marriage took place and ending with the last day of the month preceding the month in which the divorce action was filed. Some such fictitious determination was necessary to enable the Family Court to determine the precise value of a pension entitlement and to allow the adjustment to be made as part of the divorce proceedings.

In post-war Germany, all political decisions which result in new legislation must be made within the framework of the Basic Law, particularly the fundamental rights provisions. This gives the Constitutional Court an important role in the legislative process. Not surprisingly, the scheme for the adjustment of pensions enacted in 1970 was attacked before the Court as involving a taking of property without the payment of adequate compensation, forbidden by Art 14 of the Basic Law. The Constitutional Court accepted that pension entitlements, even under Germany's compulsory schemes, are a form of property and are therefore protected by Art 14. However, the Court declared the scheme to be constitutional because of the additional clause in Art 14 to the effect that property carries social obligations (BVerfG NJW 1980, 692).

Attractive though the German legislator seems to have found the extension to pensions of the accrued gains principle, the remainder of the matrimonial property rules were quite another matter. Had pensions been subjected to matrimonial property rules, the adoption of the separation of goods regime would have excluded by implication any pension sharing after the breakdown of the marriage. When old age is still decades away, this may seem unimportant, but eventually the consequences for one of the spouses could be calamitous. The sensible solution chosen by the legislator was to make the equalisation of pensions independent of the particular matrimonial property regime which applied to the parties.

Moreover, many of the rules of the community of accrued gains regime are quite unsuitable for the adjustment of pensions. The most common pensions are those paid to public servants and those payable to employees and workers under compulsory state insurance schemes; all those are governed by public law and their adjustment, irrespective of the method chosen, is bound to be a complicated administrative process requiring the cooperation of the pension authorities. An actual divorce may justify invoking such a process, but the other circumstances which trigger an equalisation of the accrued gains (supra) do not.

For these and other reasons, the German legislator was amply justified in rejecting the seemingly simple expedient of declaring pensions to be matrimonial property under the ordinary rules.

c. Pension adjustment: a regime sui generis

The legislator obviously realised that pensions are a kind of property *sui generis* and need a tailor-made solution of their own. That is what the legislation of 1970 has provided.

The regime for the adjustment of pensions shows its independence from other institutions of the family law in a number of ways. Unlike the matrimonial property regimes and maintenance obligations, it comes into play only in the context of divorce. Breakdown without divorce leaves the pension entitlement of the parties unaffected and so do the various circumstances which bring about the premature equalisation of accrued gains (supra).

The right to pension adjustment exists quite independently of the parties' matrimonial property regime. If spouses conclude a matrimonial contract agreeing upon the separation of goods regime, this does not affect by implication the right to pension adjustment. On the other hand, it is permissible to modify or completely exclude that right by contract (§ 1408 II). Like all matrimonial contracts intended to affect matrimonial property regimes, such a contract must be concluded in solemn form before a notary public (§ 1410). It is void if this form is not observed (§ 125).[28] The contract has the effect of bringing about the separation of goods, if that has not been the parties' regime already. Further, the contract is ineffective if a divorce petition is filed within a year of its conclusion. During pending divorce proceedings such a contract may only be concluded with the approval of the Family Court.

Pension adjustment is also independent of the maintenance provisions after divorce. If, after the equalisation has taken effect, the beneficiary is still not sufficiently provided for, he or she may still have a claim for supplementary maintenance against the other spouse. If the couple was well-to-do, this is a realistic possibility. Pensions tend to be modest, while a maintenance claim after divorce might be very substantial, for its extent depends upon the parties' earlier standard of living. § 1578 reads: 'The extent of maintenance depends upon the marital circumstances.' This has been called a 'living standard guarantee'.[29] One might add that courts are allowed to place limits upon the time during which maintenance is payable at this generous level.

---

28 Registration in the Matrimonial Property Register is not a prerequisite to validity – Palandt, *Bürgerliches Gesetzbuch* 56th edn (CH Beck, München, 1997) Intro 1 to § 1558.
29 Palandt, § 1578 n 3.

d. The adjustment of pensions: the implementation of the basic principle

Simple as the basic principle of sharing pensions may seem, its practical implementation has given rise to great technical problems. In trying to solve these, the German legislator has created what is probably the most complex system of rules within the ordinary civil law. The reason for the difficulties has been that the 'clean break' principle has been applied and this has required, both substantively and procedurally, an intense interaction between private law and those public law rules which govern statutory pensions. Whenever possible, it was considered desirable to transfer part of the entitlement of the spouse with the more valuable pension rights to the other in a way which ensures that (inevitably at the expense of the rights of the transferor) the transferee acquires his or her own independent pension entitlement, severed entirely from that of the transferor.

i. Private pensions

A simple example, outside the statutory schemes, might serve to illustrate this approach. Assume that H, now 40 years of age, has acquired during the marriage by private contract an annuity, payable from age 65, and that W, aged 35, has no entitlement of any kind. Assume further that the rules of the provider of the annuity allow its partial or total transfer. As in all other cases, the adjustment in this case is the responsibility of the Family Court and the applicable provision is not to be found in the Civil Code, but in § 1 of the Law for the Regulation of Hardship Arising from Pension Adjustment of 1983,[30] which reads: 'If the regulations which govern the entitlement of the spouse liable to adjustment permit it, the Family Court will establish an entitlement for the other spouse outside the system of statutory pension insurance (*Realteilung*[31]).' To a lawyer used to the precision (some Continental observers would say pedantry) of English draftsmanship, this may seem a little cryptic, but its meaning is clear enough to German lawyers. The vagueness of the provision is intended to give the Family Court and the pension provider some leeway in relation to the way in which the division is carried out. The aim is always to provide the beneficiary of the process (W in this case) with an entitlement which is tailored to his or her own requirements (eg which terminates when she dies, not when H dies) rather than contingent on those of the other spouse. The way to achieve this is, adhering to the example given, to use half the capital value of H's entitlement to establish a pension entitlement for W. Because individual requirements are different, this solution does not necessarily yield the same periodic payment for W as it does for H (differences in life expectancies etc). Other variants for the division are possible,[32] but need

---

30   Gesetz zur Regelung von Härten im Versorgungsausgleich vom 21 February 1983.
31   This is difficult to translate; it is intended to indicate that an actual division is to take place rather than some manipulation which merely has the effect of a division.
32   *Münchener Kommentar zum Bürgerlichen Gesetzbuch* 3rd edn (CH Beck, München, 1993) Appendix I to §§ 1587–1587p.

not be examined here. For the valuation of pension rights, a special regulation entitled Cash Value Regulation (*Barwertverordnung*) may have to be consulted.

A number of private pension providers have changed their rules so as to accommodate the need for this kind of pension adjustment. Life insurance companies and many professional organisations which provide pension schemes for their members (organisations of doctors, lawyers, veterinary surgeons, dentists in a number of German states) accommodate the need for this kind of system, sometimes on condition that both spouses are members or at least eligible for membership.

ii. Statutory pensions

Public service pension entitlements are administered by the salary and pension authorities (*Besoldungs- und Versorgungsstellen*), which are part of the federal and state administrations. The schemes for government and private employees are administered by a federal authority with its seat in Berlin (*Bundesversicherungsanstalt für Angestellte*). The schemes for workers are administered by similar authorities in the various states (*Landesversicherungsanstalten*). All these pension schemes are governed by public law provisions. The pensions in these schemes are usually 'dynamic', ie they are not fixed and entirely predictable, but rather move with movements in inflation and/or changes in average earnings. If necessary, the state supplements the pension funds from public revenue. Public law pensions cover almost the whole of the workforce and are much more common than private pension arrangements.

The pension adjustment system of the Code exhibits a special, perhaps a unique, interaction between private law and public law. § 1587a II no 2 is concerned with the valuation of the pension entitlements. It reads (in the translation of Goren): 'In case of annuities or expected annuities from statutory annuity insurance, the amount to be taken into account is that which would result as old-age pension at the termination of the marriage from the payment periods falling within the subsistence of the marriage without taking into account the increase factor.'

The main administering authority is the Family Court. It makes the crucial decisions, but it could neither properly prepare nor implement its decisions without the assistance of the pension authorities. If both spouses are public servants, their pensions are adjusted with the cooperation of the public service pension authorities by a process of splitting which is very similar to the splitting process applicable to private pensions which we have already examined. Legislation has made certain that the creation of a new entitlement is facilitated. Where both parties are employees, much the same applies, except that the administering authority is the *Bundesversicherungsanstalt für Angestellte*. The situation becomes more complex if one is a public servant and the other (who happens to have a less valuable entitlement) an employee. Simple splitting is now not possible, for the employee, lacking the necessary qualification of being a public servant, cannot be accommodated under the public service scheme. For this situation a process of 'quasi-splitting' has been invented. This involves the creation of a new (or additional) pension entitlement for the employee within the relevant scheme, based upon a financial adjustment which needs to take place between the two pension authorities. The detailed operation of these schemes is extremely complex (there is also 'super-splitting' and 'quasi super-splitting'); it represents a science of its own.

iii. Pension adjustment by means of obligations
Not infrequently the splitting or quasi-splitting of pensions is simply not possible. As a last resort, the Code has made provision for the adjustment by way of obligation (§ 1587f–1587o). In such situations the adjustment is made by allowing the whole of the pension to be collected by the spouse who is liable to the adjustment and then imposing an obligation upon him or her to pay over periodically the appropriate amount to the other spouse.

e. Hardship
The German system of pension adjustment deals with pensions in isolation from the remainder of the parties' property and seeks to combine a very simple basic principle with rules and methods of implementation which could not be more complex. It will come as no surprise to a lawyer to learn that such a system has given rise to many ambiguities, difficulties of application and outright injustices, which have required legislative intervention or special treatment under let-out provisions. A few examples to illustrate these difficulties will have to suffice.

If H only receives half his pension on retirement, because the other half has been transferred to W, his reduced pension may not be sufficient to enable him to continue to pay maintenance to W (assuming he is obliged to do so until she reaches pensionable age). Until she reaches pensionable age, the transfer of the pension to her will in fact disadvantage her. Such a situation is dealt with in § 5 of the Law for the Regulation of Hardship Arising from Pension Adjustment of 1983, which provides that, until W becomes entitled to pension payments, H will continue to receive his undiminished pension so as to enable him to continue to pay maintenance to W. Thus, the problems created by the divorce and the new system were solved by an adjustment of the pension rules. One might add that the extra cost of this solution was imposed upon the public purse, or, more exactly, upon the workforce and the employers who fund the statutory pension system.

To ring the changes, assume that W dies before she reaches the age at which she could claim pension payments. It now appears that H has given up a substantial part of his pension entitlement for nothing. The solution to this conundrum is contained in § 4 of the above-mentioned Law: H will receive his full pension undiminished by the splitting which the Court had ordered.

The adjustment system is best suited to housewife marriages, ie marriages in which H is employed and becomes entitled to the pension and W gives up her employment to devote herself to the home and to the children. It does not always fit other marital situations quite so well. Where both parties have worked throughout their married lives, earning at different levels, the one who is better off will argue that it was not the help of the other spouse but a greater contribution to society which resulted in unequal pensions and that inferior qualifications and not the marriage have placed the less well-earning spouse at a disadvantage. Other cases are more dramatic. The insistence of the Code on the treatment of pensions as a separate fund with its own rules for adjustment can create strange anomalies. Beitzke (at p 184) mentions the case of a wealthy spouse who relies only on accumulated assets for support. Why should he or she be entitled to a part of the pension earned by the other spouse through long years of employment?

It is for such cases that the Code provides an escape (§§ 1587c, 1587h). An adjustment of pensions is excluded according to § 1587c if the parties' financial positions, in particular the acquisition of property during the marriage, make it seem inequitable. However, circumstances may not be taken into account solely on the ground that they have caused the failure of the marriage. Further grounds for the exclusion of an adjustment are that a party has caused the pension rights to be lost in expectation of the divorce or after the divorce, or that the claimant has, during the marriage, grossly violated his or her duty to contribute to the maintenance of the family.

f. Contractual exclusion or modification of pension adjustment
German law does not force a pension adjustment upon parties who consider that they can arrive by agreement at an arrangement better suited to their circumstances. § 1587o of the Code allows them to make a contract as part of their divorce settlement which modifies the pension adjustment prescribed by the Code. Such a contract must be distinguished from the contract made under § 1408 II, which cannot be entered into when a divorce is already looming (supra c). However, both types of arrangement are hedged around with safeguards to ensure that important rights are not given away for an inadequate return. The § 1587o contract may only be concluded with the approval of the divorce court. In deciding whether to deny its approval, the court must consider the proposed maintenance, property and pension settlement as a whole and must ask whether the total package sufficiently secures the old age of the party who would benefit from the legally prescribed pension adjustment if no agreement were made. To enable the parties and the court to make a realistic assessment, the pension authorities are obliged under § 109 III of the Social Code IV to provide information about the value of the parties' pension entitlements at the time of divorce.

III. UNMARRIED RELATIONSHIPS (URs): DIVISION OF PROPERTY ON BREAKDOWN

During the last few decades, URs have become more common in Germany. In 1995 more than 1.7 million unmarried couples maintained joint residences in the Federal Republic (nearly a third of these with children). If impermanence is one of the characteristics of the UR, then marriage has become more like it. In 1960, one marriage in ten tended to end in divorce; by 1995, it had become one marriage in three. The special constitutional protection of the institution of marriage does not seem to have had much effect.

It may be that URs tend to be different from marriages. They may have fewer children, and the housewife marriage may have fewer counterparts among the URs. Nevertheless, the break-up of a UR after many years may leave the weaker of the two partners no less exposed to difficulties than is the weaker of the two marriage partners. There might be a case for granting them equal legal protection and the easiest way would be to treat the UR as if it were a marriage.

1. The constitutional dimension

If a stable UR which has lasted for some time and has, perhaps, resulted in children, were to be regarded as a 'marriage' under Art 6 of the Basic Law (which places marriage and the family under the particular protection of the state), equal treatment would not only be facilitated, it would be constitutionally required. Constitutional principles should move with the times to some extent, but at this stage, there would hardly be a single voice in Germany which would defend such a proposition. The Constitutional Court has repeatedly made it clear that only a relationship which is *öffentlich feststellbar* (ascertainable because of official publicity) can be regarded as a marriage.[33] The constitutional equality principle (Art 3) might be invoked to demand that the legislator treat marriage and URs alike, but the Constitutional Court has rejected such arguments: 'The legislator is at liberty to attach a different set of legal consequences to the free and responsible decision which has been made by the partners in a UR not to enter into a marriage from those which attach to a validly concluded marital relationship with its manifold rights and obligations.'[34] Hausmann has asked whether the principles of the rule of law and of social justice do not imply a constitutional requirement to offer some kind of protection to the weaker of the partners in such a relationship when the other partner engages in exploitation and sharp practice.[35] His answer is that constitutional intervention (ie intervention by the Constitutional Court) would only be justified if the ordinary courts proved unable to offer a

---

33 Decisions of 24 March 1981 (BVerfGE 56, 363, 386) and of 30 November 1982 (BVerfGE 62, 323, 330).
34 Decision of 1 June 1983 (FamRZ 1983, 1211).
35 *Nichteheliche Lebensgemeinschaften und Vermögensausgleich* (München, 1989).

modicum of protection by applying or moulding existing legal principles. Controversy about these matters, despite the relative freedom to deal with them which the legislator in Germany has enjoyed, has not been very vigorous (as it has been in England, France or Scandinavia), for some of the constitutional and other arguments against equating marriage and URs have been considered rather weighty and have suppressed debate.

If the constitutional dykes are to be breached, it will have to happen by invoking the family concept, not that of marriage. It is well established in constitutional law that 'family' in Art 6 is the nuclear family, not the extended one,[36] and that the relationships between mother and child[37] on the one hand and between father and child[38] on the other (at least if father and child live together) fall within this concept and that they enjoy corresponding constitutional protection. Because the partners in an intact UR are not in a marriage, a grotesque situation exists when there is a child, for, in the eyes of the Constitution, they are two families. Not surprisingly, legal writers tend to plead for an end to such nonsense. Even if the Constitutional Court were to take this step, it would still not turn URs into marriages. It also remains clear that the childless UR is not a family, even if the partners have undertaken by contract some of the duties which flow from a marriage.

Article 6 is not the only constitutional provision which has a bearing upon URs. There is also Art 2 I, which gives every person the right to the unimpeded development of his or her personality. The Constitutional Court has recognised that this implies the right to form unions which do not conform to the traditional pattern of the marriage relationship. It follows that Art 6 does not prohibit URs. Marriage as an institution is protected, but not against 'competition' from other forms of union. On the other hand, one could not equate marriages and URs by legislation, for this would negate the 'particular' protection which the state owes to marriage.

As things stand constitutionally, none of the principles which have been explained as applicable to marriage are directly applicable to URs. This does not preclude the possibility that the operation of other principles may sometimes generate similar results.

2. The public policy dimension

The legal treatment of URs depends not only upon constitutional considerations. There is also a non-constitutional public policy dimension. Before legal rights of a private law character can be attached to facts with a strong UR component, the law must first decide its outlook on sex outside marriage. The prevailing view used to be that such relations were against good morals, a view

---

36 Decision of 29 July 1959 (BVerfGE 10, 59, 66).
37 Decision of 23 October 1958 (BVerfGE 8, 210, 215).
38 Decision of 8 June 1977 (BVerfGE 45, 104, 123) and decision of 24 March 1981 (BVerfGE 56, 363, 382 et seq).

which used to lead to the invalidity of testamentary bequests for the benefit of lovers and of contracts of all sorts in which a sexual relationship was a significant element.[39] Many voices in the popular press and in legal literature attacked such views, rejecting any suggestion that long-standing and serious relationships with a sexual component were no better than prostitution. The *Zeitgeist* was decidedly against the older outlook and caused the courts to change their tune. URs are now regarded as involving an acceptable alternative life style. It has been held that the letting of an apartment to an unmarried couple is legally unobjectionable.[40] To be sure, contracts involving prostitution pure and simple continue to be regarded as invalid.

The change in the outlook of the courts has meant that partners in a UR are free to regulate their relationship, either comprehensively or in particular respects by contract.

3. The case for legal intervention after the break-up of URs

There can be no doubt that in many cases involving the break-up of a UR, some kind of adjustment of the parties' property relations is called for. Hausmann has made the case for such an approach very convincingly:

> 'Between the partners of *Lebensgemeinschaften* ('life partnerships') considerable shifts in the formal ownership of property often take place without a positive intention thereby to augment the property position of one or the other partner in any definitive way. Whether a thing belongs to one or the other, its use will continue to be available to both without regard to the question of formal ownership. It follows that parties should, after break-up, not necessarily be allowed to put forward the formal position as the one which should remain the final one between them.'

The important questions are: How far should legal intervention in such cases go? By what legal means is it to be achieved?

i. Analogy to marriage

If the UR cannot be given a marriage-like status by constitutional interpretation or family law principles, one might turn to the law of contract to achieve a similar result. In 1978 an argument was put forward by Roth-Stielow[41] to the effect that 'moving in together' amounted to the tacit conclusion of a contract *sui generis* which obliged the parties to live together, love and be faithful to each other and render each other mutual assistance. Such an approach might have provided a satisfactory basis for a just solution of the

---

39   The basic premise of the courts was that 'in principle sexual relations between unmarried persons are contrary to good morals and so is *a fortiori* intercourse with someone other than his or her marriage partner' – Federal Supreme Court of Justice, decision of 26 February 1968 (JZ 1968, 468). For examples from post-war German case-law, see Hausmann p 52.
40   Decision of the Federal Supreme Court of Justice of 3 October 1984 (BGHZ 92, 219).
41   JR 1978, 233–236.

property and maintenance problems arising on break-up of the relationship, but it flew in the face of the frequently undoubted intention of both, or at least of one, of the parties to avoid the legal consequences of marriage. On a more legalistic level, the legal world in Germany rejected the suggestion with the argument that the law recognised only one union of this type, ie marriage, and that it had conclusively regulated its incidents.

ii. Other legal tools, particularly the law of contract

Another approach is to invoke the provisions of the Code about partnerships or associations of the civil law (as distinct from those governed by the Commercial Code) (§§ 705–740). § 705 reads: 'The parties to an association contract enter into a mutual agreement to seek to achieve a common object in a manner specified in the contract, particularly to render the agreed contributions.' The rejection of Roth-Stielow's argument does not preclude seeing a UR as based on an implied contract to live together for the time being, thus creating a legal framework in which all aspects of the relationship, including its liquidation after a break-up, could be legally regulated.

The courts would not go so far as to imply a mutual agreement that each party should have authority to represent the other in the administration of matters of common concern. However, even without such authority, there can still be what German lawyers call an *'Innengesellschaft'* (partnership or association with internal effect only). It has been defined as a partnership whereby the partners have undertaken to pursue a common aim together, but where authority to act for both is lacking, and where, therefore, each partner can only act for himself or herself as against third parties.[42] This concept is somewhat remindful of the silent partnership. It is accepted in German law as an institution of the private law, so that it can operate outside the purely commercial sphere.

According to the prevailing view, there are three reasons why joining together in a UR cannot be considered a sufficient common purpose. First, it is thought that it is insufficiently specific as a purpose. Secondly, it is considered that it contains too many purely personal elements which are not relevant to the economic aspect of the relationship and that this aspect is the only which is legally relevant. Finally, recognition of this as a common purpose would establish a kind of minor rival to the institution of marriage, which would be contrary to public policy.[43]

The Federal Supreme Court of Justice has given the green light to the use of the device of the 'internal partnership', provided the partners in a UR could be said to have combined, not just to live together, but to acquire or establish particular assets of economic value, which they intend to use jointly during their partnership, and which they envisage as common property, even if that

---

42 Palandt, § 705, n 26.
43 For a review of these arguments, see Münchener Kommentar, Appendix to § 1302, nn 17–20.

does not accord with the strict rules of the law of property (BGHZ 77, 55). Examples of objects acquired and owned on this basis, and recognised as joint by the courts, have been *inter alia* a manufacturing business,[44] a hotel,[45] and a house.[46] In an internal partnership, the mere fact that such an object is legally owned by only one of the partners, and that that partner conducts himself or herself as sole proprietor, is not necessarily an obstacle to a finding that an internal partnership has come into being. This limited recognition of the partnership concept is a far cry from the treatment of marriage, not least because the finding that a partnership has existed can never be taken for granted. There are numerous cases in which, for one reason or another, such a finding was not made.[47] This gives the partners in URs no real assurance that their relations will be dealt with appropriately if their relationship should fail. Where a finding recognising an implied partnership is made, provisions concerning the termination and liquidation of the relationship are to be found in §§ 732–735, which lead to satisfactory results.

The rules concerning internal partnerships are not the only tools which can be used to distribute property in a satisfactory manner. The rules concerning unjust enrichment and those of the law of property may also yield fair results in some cases. According to the law of property, the acquisition of household goods paid for by one of the partners does not necessarily result in joint ownership. However, when both parties possess the item, the Code invokes a presumption of joint ownership, which it may not be very easy to rebut.[48] This also affords some protection of the partners in a UR.

IV. THE GERMAN SYSTEM: SOME PERSONAL VIEWS
1. Marriage

The basic policy judgments implicit in the design of the German system may be summed up as follows:

(a) According to the German legal tradition, which deserves to be continued, property relations between marriage partners are not left to the ordinary law of property, but are governed by special matrimonial property regimes.

(b) Marriage partners are not to be forced into one rigid system, but must be given some limited choice of regime. One option should be the sharing of the bulk of their property (with the possibility of moulding their regime to their particular circumstances), another the avoidance of any kind of

---

44 BGHZ 84, 388.
45 OLG Hamm, NJW 80, 1530.
46 BGH, FamRZ 1992, 408.
47 Establishment of a bank account in the name of only one of the partners (OLG Düsseldorf, NJW 79, 1509); renovation of a rented farmhouse (OLG München, FamRZ 88, 58).
48 §§ 866, 1006, 1008 and OLG Düsseldorf, NJW 92, 1706.

sharing (total separation). Because of the importance of such agreements, they must be made in solemn form (eg before a notary public).
(c) In the large majority of cases no choice will have been made. For these a standardised solution (with its inherent advantages, to the parties and the courts, of certainty and predictability), combined with a let-out clause for cases of gross unfairness, is appropriate, rather than solutions which are made to depend on all the circumstances of individual cases.

This judgment has been vindicated by subsequent developments, for breakdown of marriage has become a mass phenomenon and individualised solutions would now be beyond the reach of the legal system. Some standardisation might have grown out of judicial practice, but the ministerial officials who drew up the system did not want to leave things to chance.

(d) The standardised solution most in harmony with the ideal of marriage as a cooperative relationship is the equal sharing of gains, limited to those which accrued during the marriage.

The limitation has also been vindicated by subsequent developments, for short-term marriages have become much more common. They could now hardly be dealt with as if they had been long-term unions.

(e) The most effective way of achieving the actual sharing of accrued gains is the imposition of an 'equalisation claim', involving simply the payment of money after breakdown. The possible alternative, the sharing of actual items of property, would be legally unduly complex.
(f) Pensions are a form of property and should be shared equally like other accrued gains (with the same limitation), but they are so important that they deserve a regime of their own, exempt from both the general and the matrimonial property rules. Pension entitlements should be shared irrespective of the property regime which applies to the particular marriage. A standardised solution combined with a let-out clause is again appropriate and no administrative effort should be spared in making the sharing principle effective. Its exclusion by contract (while still possible) should be made particularly difficult.

2. Unmarried relationships

URs have become an important social phenomenon in the last few decades. The problems arising upon the breakdown of such relationships require a response from the legal system which is no less carefully planned and executed than is the response to the breakdown of marriage. Nothing remotely similar has been attempted. Instead, the problems have been left to the courts including the Constitutional Court.

(a) The UR is now recognised as a union to be accepted as a legitimate 'competitor' of marriage. Past attitudes of active judicial disapproval have been abandoned.

(b) Constitutional principles derived from Art 6 of the Basic Law probably prohibit such treatment of URs (particularly such protection of the weaker of the two parties) as would in effect equate URs with marriages.

This seems to show how well-intentioned constitutional principles and particularly fundamental constitutional rights sometimes turn into obstacles to justice and to sensible social policy when social conditions and attitudes undergo change.

(c) Because the rules which apply to marriage cannot be applied to URs, and because there are no separate principles specifically designed to deal fairly with the division of property, including pensions, upon breakdown, the actual solutions reached in the courts have been left to the general law, in particular the laws of contract, unjust enrichment and property.

The legal treatment of URs has one particularly unfortunate feature. Many of the rules which apply to marriage are so designed as to lend themselves particularly well to analogical application to URs. Although the absence of a vow of life-long solidarity genuinely distinguishes URs from marriages, only a very few of the rules which govern marriage are in fact based upon this distinction. The limitation of the sharing of gains and of pensions to the period during which a marriage persisted make the actual partnership between the parties the essential criterion and that very often exists between partners in an unmarried relationship in exactly the same way. Reform is badly needed but will be difficult to achieve because of constitutional impediments.

Chapter 4

STRENGTHS AND WEAKNESSES OF THE LAW ON PENSION SPLITTING IN THE UNITED KINGDOM

Robin Ellison

INTRODUCTION

It is now required[1] that pension rights should be taken into account by advisers and the court when reviewing division of matrimonial property on divorce. Two main problems have emerged in practice:

(1) whether the statutory valuation as set down in the relevant regulations[2] is appropriate in the circumstances, and
(2) once the valuation is agreed, which method of settlement is appropriate.

But there are other, more academic issues as well. The question of settlement method is a relatively new one, for cases in which petitions were issued before 1 July 1996 there was only one method. Now there are two, and shortly there will be three. They are as follows:

(1) *set-off*, as before, readjusting the division of matrimonial assets to take account of pension rights;
(2) *earmarking*, ie an order of the court directing that part or all of any lump sum or pension arising at retirement be paid to the other spouse; and
(3) *sharing* (or *splitting*), ie an order of the court directing the pension scheme to allocate part or all of the pension rights to be awarded to the other spouse at divorce. This is provided for in principle under ss 16 and 17 of the Family Law Act 1996, but is unlikely to be operative for some time yet.

There are both theoretical and practical problems in the application and development of these remedies. In order to clarify the issues, it may be helpful first to explore the rather arcane UK pension system.

---

1   Matrimonial Causes Act 1973, s 25B as inserted by the Pensions Act 1995.
2   Divorce etc (Pensions) Regulations 1996, SI 1996/1676; Family Proceedings (Amendment) (No 2) Rules 1996, SI 1996/1674; Pensions Act 1995 (Commencement) (No 5) Order 1996, 1996/1675; Divorce etc (Pensions) (Amendment) Regulations 1997, SI 1997/636; Family Proceedings (Amendment) Rules 1997, SI 1997/637 (revoking Family Proceedings (Amendment) (No 3) Rules, 1996, SI 1996/1778).

THE UK PENSION SYSTEM

The UK pension system is one of the most complex in the world. It is useful to categorise it into state benefits, personal benefits and company-backed benefits, although the boundaries between these categories are sometimes blurred.

State benefits

There are two state pension arrangements:

(1) The *basic state pension* provides a maximum of around £62 per week for a single person, provided he has a full employment record. Since this is payable as a social security benefit, and the courts have no jurisdiction over social security, it is not normally taken account of in divorce matters. In any event, a divorced former wife (although not a divorced former husband) can use a former husband's earnings record to enjoy a pension in her own right. The basic state pension is therefore in practice ignored in divorce arrangements.

(2) The *additional state pension* ('SERPS' (State Earnings Related Pension Scheme)) provides around 20% of earnings up to around £24,000 per annum. On divorce, however, the spouse cannot use the earner's track record to enjoy a parallel state benefit; it is therefore lost to the spouse. The benefits can either be provided:
   – by the state (in which case the scheme is 'contracted-in'); or
   – privately by an employer's pension scheme (in which case the scheme is 'contracted-out') or through an individual's personal pension (in which case it is an 'appropriate personal pension').

In practice, few individuals are aware of what the SERPS pension will provide, since the rules are complicated. The level of benefits can be ascertained by asking the DSS.[3] If the benefits are provided through a company or personal pension scheme, they are conventionally included in the ordinary valuation and not separately identified.

There is a major constitutional issue which the development of this rather peculiar system has thrown up. In general, social security benefits are not subject to the jurisdiction of the family courts. Social security benefits, if they are anything, could be regarded as benefits *in personam* rather than a benefit *in rem*. Accordingly, for example, the courts would have no jurisdiction over contracted-in benefits, but would over contracted-out benefits. This would have a minor tendency amongst divorcing people towards contracting back in the state scheme, to oust the jurisdiction of the courts, and reverse the objectives of government which for demographic reasons is trying to persuade the population to leave the state arrangements.

---

3   See Form BR19 from the DSS.

Occupational and personal pensions

Private pensions can either be provided:[4]

(1) individually, either:
   - by the individual contributing (perhaps with additional contributions by his employer, if any) to a personal pension scheme (perhaps with an insurance company or bank or building society); or
   - by an employer making contributions to a company scheme, (perhaps with contributions by the employee); or
(2) collectively, by the employer providing benefits as set out in a 'defined-benefits' scheme, with contributions made preponderantly or solely by the employer, sometimes with contributions, or added contributions, by the employee.

Money purchase and final salary

In considering the division of pension rights, it is essential to determine just what those rights are.

(1) *Defined contribution schemes.* In some schemes ('defined-contribution' or 'money-purchase' schemes) the benefits are merely what can be provided by a sum of money accumulated over time. The accumulated sum is used at retirement to buy a pension. The value depends on what annuity rates are at that time, and whether the value of the accumulated sum is affected by for example a fall or rise in the stock market at the time it is cashed in to buy an annuity.
(2) *Defined benefit schemes.* In other schemes (which must be employer-related), the amount of money in the scheme is not relevant; the promise is of a benefit, perhaps related to salary. For example the promise by the employer may be to provide half-salary or two-thirds salary. The promise is built up over years, perhaps at $\frac{1}{60}$ of salary for each year of employment, so that after 40 years' employment the employee will be entitled to $\frac{40}{60}$ of his salary at retirement (ie $\frac{2}{3}$). Such benefits may be index-linked, and with additional benefits sometimes at the discretion of the scheme's trustees. Until recently there was no need to have such promises by an employer supported by financial guarantees. From April 1997 the law required such promises to be supported by funds in a pension scheme.[5]

---

[4] There is no shortage of general commentaries of the UK pensions system, especially the legal aspects of it; see eg Ellison, *Pensions Law and Practice*, 3 vols looseleaf (Sweet & Maxwell); Ellison, *The Pensions Practice* (Pendragon); *Pensions in Practice* (IDS Pensions Service).

[5] At least in relation to salaries over a certain level, known as the earnings cap. It is index-linked; in 1998/99, it is £87,600, a little over $100,000.

Funded and unfunded schemes

While money-purchase schemes are by definition funded, defined benefit schemes often do not have enough funds to pay all benefits if the schemes were closed tomorrow. There are many good reasons for this:

(1) the assets may have fallen in value at the time the scheme was closed, although in normal circumstances they would have been enough;
(2) interest rates had fallen at the time although that was not reasonably expected, or promises had been made that would have been paid for over the years, but not enough time has passed.

In addition:

(3) it is not normally tax effective to provide assets to support promises for pensions in respect of income over the 'earnings cap'.[6] In other words, tax relief is not available to pension funds in relation to incomes over this level;
(4) many perfectly proper pension schemes are not funded; these include many schemes in the public sector (among them, the Civil Service, teachers, police and firemen). It is calculated that the Civil Service scheme will have to find around £500 million a year of money it does not have when it has to pay capital sums to divorced spouses on divorce.[7]

The protection of such rights for spouses is therefore less effective; if the payments are dependant on the future survival of the employer, they may be less attractive and certainly harder to enforce.

Discretionary and indexed benefits

In final-salary or salary-related systems, some benefits are available as of right (subject to sufficient assets being available), and others may or may not be available, depending again on resources and the views of the trustees or managers. When valuing benefits it is not always clear whether these discretionary benefits (which may include for example benefits on ill-health, or early-retirement benefits or inflation-protection) are to be included or not.

---

6   See note 5 supra.
7   This figure is anecdotal within the industry, but seems reasonable. See, for example, Dnes, *The Division of Marital Assets following Divorce with Particular Reference to Pensions*, Lord Chancellor's Department Research Secretariat, December 1997, No 7/97, which also has a small useful bibliography.

VALUATION

Introduction

In practice, one of the major difficulties is the valuation of both the member's and the spouse's rights. Both need to be valued separately.[8]

Member's valuations

The value of a member's or an employee's rights in a money-purchase pension system is (theoretically) relatively easy to identify; it is (except as below) the value of the assets standing to his credit. The value of an employee's interests in a final-salary is more difficult to define, since it involves the application of actuarial techniques, identifying the value of the underlying guarantee, and the impact of the imprecise value of discretionary benefits. There is however a standard valuation technique, called a 'cash-equivalent', based on recommended actuarial guidance, which is used by the regulations. This is discussed below.

Spouse's valuations

The value of a spouse's rights is a proportion of a member's rights.

But a spouse's interest is in several parts, particularly in respect of salary-related schemes:

(1) the survivor's rights, which will disappear by virtue of any divorce; and
(2) the interest in the member's rights which he will enjoy once the benefit is in payment.

There will be some actuarial interest in discretionary or contingent benefits; but lump sums (except as a means of future payment) are only a different way of expressing a pension benefit (this is slightly different in the case of some public sector schemes).

The interest will be affected or can be affected by a number of elements including:

(1) the life expectancy of the member; if that is impaired, the spouse's interest will be greater;
(2) the difference in ages of the spouses; if the spouse is much younger, her interest could be greater.

It is often convenient to express a spouse's rights as a percentage of a member's rights.

Methods available

There are many ways of valuing a member's interests.

---

8   For a superb US study, written in a relaxed rather than academic style, see Shulman and Kelley, *Dividing Pensions in Divorce* (John Wiley, 1996).

In money purchase cases the value of the account is often easy to determine. But even here, there may be a different value depending on whether the funds are left with the investment manager or insurer (the 'fund value') or whether the policy is to be paid up or surrendered (the 'surrender value'), which could be very substantially less.

In defined-benefit cases, as well as the problems of what benefits to take into account, and the variability of the personal factors, there are problems of assumptions. There are two main assumption problems:

(1) the fact that assumptions as to future interest rates, income rates and annuity rates can be difficult to agree. Few can guess as to future inflation rates for example; and low future inflation could double the value of a benefit compared with high future inflation. Different actuaries will have different expectations about these future rates, and small differences in assumptions can cause major differences in valuations. It is sensible to use mid-range assumptions, regardless of whether the valuation is prepared for the petitioner or the respondent, but in particular cases these may not be appropriate.
(2) the fact that defined-benefit schemes often contain reserves designed to cope with the fact that a member may continue in employment with the company and that he may enjoy salary increases and career progression increases. If the member leaves before they come into play, those reserves are no longer required.

It is therefore possible to value the same pension rights in many different ways; it may be helpful to refer to just three:

(1) past service reserves, which include the reserves mentioned above;
(2) transfer values (or sometimes cash equivalents), a statutory minimum valuation, which does not take into account these reserves; or
(3) share of fund which, if there is a significant surplus in the fund, may be higher than the first two (or lower, if there is a deficit in the fund).

Cash equivalent transfer value

The regulations (the Divorce etc (Pensions) Regulations 1996) require that the valuation method used in the proceedings is the cash equivalent transfer value (CETV). It was the method recommended by the Pensions Management Institute/Law Society Working Party Report of 1993. Its advantage is that it is cheap (free) to the parties and readily calculable by pension schemes.[9]

---

9   The arguments for the use of this system was set out in a series of preliminary documents; see, eg, Department of Social Security, *The Treatment of Pension Rights on Divorce*, Cm 3345 (London, HMSO, 1996); Prior and Field, *Pensions and Divorce*, Report No 5, Department of Social Security (London, HMSO, 1996); Foster and Freed, *Women and Pensions*, Department of Social Security, Report No 49 (London, HMSO, 1996).

But where the parties have been married for some time, or the earnings are higher, such a valuation can be misleading, sometimes by a factor of four or five. In such cases, it is crucial and prudent to use a different system, perhaps the past service reserve approach, which may be more appropriate. It certainly enables the solicitor to give proper advice on which method of settlement should be employed.

The CETV used is not identical to that used to calculate transfers when leaving a scheme; it is reduced by the value of the survivor's benefit.

A major problem and drawback of the CETV however is that in practice it is more favourable to the earner or member than to the spouse; it is the method of valuation that produces the lowest figure.

JURISDICTION OF THE COURT

Since 1 July 1996 the court has had power to make an order in respect of pensions. In relation to petitions issued before July although it was settled law that the court could take pensions into account when considering financial arrangements on divorce (and in Scotland had to consider pensions)[10] in practice the law throughout the UK was constrained by the fact that the courts had no authority to direct pension scheme managers and trustees to allocate one spouse's interests or part of them to another. In practice, there were two main problems:

(1) the court had no power to make an order in relation to a member's pension rights; and
(2) it was difficult in some cases for a spouse's advisers to obtain the information.

Protective trusts

There were three main reasons for the court's previous difficulties:

(1) the Inland Revenue require as a condition of approval of the scheme that it contains a clause against 'alienation', prohibiting a member charging or alienating his acquired pension interests to anyone else;
(2) the Inland Revenue rules as set down in statute and in practice notes prohibit the allocation of a member's pension rights to a spouse;[11]

---

10 For Scotland the situation differs slightly with, some say, a distinction without a difference. See, eg, *Pension Sharing on Divorce in the Scottish Context* (The Scottish Office, February 1998). Cf a decision of the New York Summary Suffolk County Supreme Court, *Massaro v Massaro* (*New York Law Journal*, 26 December 1997), which discusses whether a spouse is entitled to a share of a pension increase arising out of the member's promotion after the petition was served.
11 Cf Inland Revenue Practice Notes IR12 1997 edition, para 2.9.

(3) almost all occupational schemes and an increasing number of personal pensions contain 'protective trusts' or 'spendthrift trusts' which operate a form of 'Catch-22' system. It operates so that where a court makes an order against a member, the member's rights in a scheme will be forfeit, and the trustees then decide to whom to make payments – which can include the member himself. In practice, it makes it all but impossible to obtain garnishee orders against such payments, so that to all intents and purposes the protective trust mechanism is effective as protection. From 1 July 1996 the court has had power to overcome these trusts in relation to divorce matters.

Obtaining information

It is now much easier than before to obtain information about pension arrangements. A member would normally disclose in his affidavit of means (or if not would be asked about them) details of pension arrangements.

Once that information is available, it is normally possible to obtain the necessary further information to value the member's interests:

(1) under the Disclosure Regulations[12] under which some consider a spouse has rights to a member's pensions information; or
(2) under an order under the Family Proceedings Rules[13] for a production order. This may be necessary especially where the scheme is a personal pension scheme; or
(3) under the Divorce etc (Pensions) Regulations 1996[14] which grant specific power to grant information to the member. Oddly, the regulations do not grant power to the spouse although the Information Regulations probably do. Unfortunately most schemes do not accept (probably wrongly) the right of spouses to such information direct.

Making the spouse a scheme member – the *Brooks* case

There has been some confusion about the relevance of the decision in *Brooks v Brooks*.[15] The decision on *Brooks* suggested that the court may in some cases have jurisdiction under the Matrimonial Causes Act 1973 to reallocate pension rights between husband and wife. The House of Lords decision seems to apply only in relatively infrequent cases:

(1) in the absence of protective trusts; and
(2) where an order would not affect third party rights, ie where the only member is the respondent; and

---

12 Occupational Pension Schemes (Disclosure of Information) Regulations 1996, SI 1996/1718, and see the Pensions Act 1995, s 133.
13 Family Proceedings Rules, r 2.63.
14 Regulation 4.
15 *Brooks v Brooks* [1996] AC 375, [1995] 3 All ER 257, [1995] 3 WLR 141, [1995] 3 FCR 214, [1995] 2 FLR 13, [1995] Fam Law 545, [1995] Pensions Law Reports 173, HL.

(3) where the scheme is in surplus; and
(4) where the spouse was employed by the same employer; and
(5) where the scheme was established under trust (not always the case in personal pension arrangements).

In practice therefore it seems limited to certain rare small self-administered pension schemes, a special form of pension scheme appropriate to small family companies. In any event the impact of the Matrimonial Causes Act 1973, s 25B suggests that such orders will not normally be considered by the courts in future. This paper therefore does not deal with it further.

The changes

It was recommended by the Pensions Management Institute/Law Society report in May 1993[16] and the Goode Committee Report on pensions law reform in September 1993[17] that the law be reformed to allow the court to grant in some cases a 'Pensions Adjustment Order' directing the trustees or managers to reallocate pensions interests. The reform suggested was of 'pensions splitting' (ie division at divorce) rather than 'earmarking' (ie orders to take effect at retirement).

The White Paper in June 1994[18] indicated that for various reasons reform was not to be expected for some time; however the Family Law Act 1996 introduced the concept in ss 16 and 17. For technical reasons it requires further primary legislation before it can be fully implemented. Proposals for such legislation are now contained in *Pension Sharing on Divorce: Reforming Pensions for a Fairer Future*.[19]

Meanwhile, the law was changed following substantial pressure for reform during the passage of the Pensions Act 1995, which introduced the concept of earmarking to the Matrimonial Causes Act 1973. In particular, ss 25B–25D of the MCA 1973 gives the courts power:

(1) to award a periodical payments order against the pension when in payment; and/or
(2) to compel a member to take such commutation of pension rights as is available and transfer some or all of it to the spouse; and/or
(3) to require scheme trustees to pay part or all of any death-in-service lump sums to the spouse, overriding any nomination letters.

---

16 Pensions Management Institute and Law Society, *Pensions and Divorce*, report of an independent working party (PMI, May 1993).
17 Pensions Law Reform Committee, Report (HMSO, September 1993) paras 4.16 et seq.
18 Department of Social Security *Pensions: Treatment of Pension Rights on Divorce*, Cm 3345 (HMSO, July 1996) (Green Paper); see also Department of Social Security *Pension Rights on Divorce*, Cm 3564 (HMSO, February 1997).
19 DSS, June 1998. Draft legislation is contained in Part 2.

The periodical payments orders come to an end on the death of either of the parties or on remarriage of the spouse. The principles underlying the regulations were set out in a summary paper issued by the Lord Chancellor's Department in June 1996 and still used in practice, although the Department now considers it outdated.[20]

PROBLEMS WITH THE VALUATION

Obtaining the CETV for both the member's and the spouse's pensions interests is only part of the process. In the absence of reallocation of the pension (which even now may not be the preferred route since a clean break is still the optimum solution) the value must be split on the time-honoured basis of adjusting the rest of the matrimonial property. The CETV is the only value to be placed in the documents available to the court;[21] it is not usually however the right value to be used in advising clients whether to seek a set-off or an earmarking order. Nor is it the right value to use in deciding what level of settlement to advise in either case.

The reason for the inadequacy of the CETV is set out below; in carrying out the negotiations on behalf of the client the following will be taken into account:

Variability of valuations

A valuation is a matter of art rather than of science; for example:

(1) in a money-purchase scheme, the CETV uses the surrender value of the policy; this can in practice be very much less than the fund value and misleading in particular circumstances; and
(2) in a defined-benefit scheme the figure will vary according to the assumptions made, the method of valuation, the importance of any discretionary and contingent benefits and the extent of the spouse's interest. The CETV assumes that the member will leave the scheme at the time of divorce; this will give a much lower valuation than using an assumption that he will stay in the scheme until retirement. Furthermore the CETV does not take into account death benefits or discretionary benefits.

Accordingly, it is usually sensible to obtain a further independent valuation on the basis that the member will continue in service; the correct figure to use in negotiations will therefore be somewhere between the two extremes.

---

20 Lord Chancellor's Department, Summary Paper, 'The provisions of the regulations under section 166 of the Pensions Act 1995' (Family Policy Division, June 1996).
21 Affidavit of means or Form D43D.

Negotiating a set-off

When deciding whether to seek a set-off solution rather than an earmarking solution, the following will normally be considered:

Tax

Whatever is agreed as the member's value, and then whatever is agreed as the spouse's percentage of that value, the agreed figure should be adjusted to take account of the fact that it will be settled without any tax obligation; normally pensions bear tax of between 23% and 40% although sometimes some of it can be commuted tax-free.

Discount for cash

A spouse may also wish to give a further allowance for the fact that a benefit is being acquired in cash, rather than later in the form of pension.

Discount for early payment

A spouse may also wish to give a further allowance for the fact that a benefit is being acquired now rather than some years in the future.

Discount for risk

A spouse may also wish to give a further allowance for the fact that a benefit is being acquired which is certain, rather than subject to the vagaries of risk to the investments of the funds, the risks of death of either the member or the spouse or both, the risks of tax changes, and other risks.

Setting-off of own pension arrangements

Spouses will be aware that whatever applies to a member's pension rights will also apply to their own.

Pensions for house and 'grave hardship' practice

In the past the practice has often been to adjust a spouse's interest in the proceedings of the matrimonial home in lieu of being able to settle the pension rights. This practice will no doubt continue but spouses will be aware that sometimes there is insufficient equity in the house to do this. In the case especially of lower-earners with significant pension rights it may even now be appropriate to defer a divorce until the pension is in payment, and then obtain a maintenance order rather than seek an earmarking order, in order to preserve a spousal pension.

Earmarking

Earmarking allows the court to make an order addressed to the trustees or managers of a pension scheme directing them at the time the member begins to draw benefits:

(1) to pay some or all of any lump sum (such as a death-in-service benefit, or a commutation of a part of the pension) to the spouse; an order can require a spouse to commute;
(2) to pay some or all of any pension to the spouse.

The lump sum payments are treated as capital payments and thus survive the death or remarriage of the spouse. The pension payments do not survive death of either party or remarriage of the spouse.

The order can be made in percentage terms or in money terms. The draftsman of the orders will need to bear in mind that the tax is paid by the member before payment, that tax rates may change, and that life expectancies or the desire to remarry will affect the decision. The use of the CETV, in deciding whether cash adjustments or earmarking is preferable, will be misleading.

In any event the spouse will need to consider insuring the member against death before the spouse, since the pension payments will cease on the member's death. In addition, pension arrangements will need to be considered for the spouse. In due course it is expected that non-earners will be able to make contributions to pension schemes. That is not presently possible.

THE PRESENT SYSTEM IN PRACTICE

Earmarking and pre-Pensions Act divorces

The earmarking provisions apply to petitions for divorce, judicial separation or nullity on or after 1 July 1996, where the prescribed notice of application has been filed on or after 1 August 1996.[22] Where the petition was issued on or after 1 July 1996 and the prescribed notice of application has been filed before 1 August 1996 the notice of application may be amended on or after 1 August 1996 so as to include provision under the Matrimonial Causes Act 1973, ss 25B or 25C.[23] Leave is not required for such an amendment. Where the petition for divorce, nullity or judicial separation was issued before 1 July 1996, the Pensions Act 1995, s 166 does not apply to any answer or cross-petition filed in the proceedings.[24]

---

22 Pensions Act 1995 (Commencement) (No 5) Order 1996, SI 1996/1775.
23 Pensions Act 1995 (Commencement) (No 5) Order 1996, art 4; Family Proceedings (Amendment) (No 2) Rules 1996, SI 1996/1674, r 3.
24 Pensions Act 1995 (Commencement) (No 5) Order 1996, art 4(2).

If a scheme member issued a petition immediately before 1 July 1996 in order to pre-empt the spouse from invoking the new earmarking provisions; a spouse could consider issuing a further petition and leave is not required. The court may order consolidation.[25] A spouse who issued his or her own petition before 1 July 1996 may apply to have the petition dismissed, although it could be argued that it is an abuse of process.

Orders available

The court may make an order that:

(1) the pension scheme trustees or managers pay all or part of the member's pension to his spouse as a periodical payment order. Such an order will come into effect only when a party with pension rights takes his pension. It comes to an end when the pension scheme member dies. The court cannot direct when the scheme member should retire;
(2) the scheme member commutes his pension benefits up to the lump sum maximum allowed by the pension scheme on retirement and that the scheme pays all or part of that benefit to the former spouse;
(3) (in respect of any death in service benefits) that the pension scheme pay all or part of the death benefits to the other party.

These are varieties of periodical payments orders and lump sum orders and unless otherwise provided have the same characteristics. Earmarking orders are only effective where there are benefits to meet them. They cannot be made so that the scheme has to pay more than is available for payment to an individual pension scheme member.

Application for an earmarking order

The court cannot make an order of its own motion, and an application must be made.[26] The petition needs to include a claim for the usual forms of ancillary relief, but a specific claim for an earmarking order does not have to be made in the petition itself.

The application should be made on Form M11 or M13 in non-pilot scheme courts and in pilot scheme courts on Form A.

The application must be served on the pension scheme trustees or managers.

They must also be provided with the following information:

(1) an address to which any notice which the trustees or managers are required to serve under the Divorce etc (Pensions) Regulations 1996 is to be sent;

---

25 Hallam, 'Earmarking – avoiding the 1 July 1996 barrier', [1997] Fam Law 267.
26 Family Proceedings Rules 1991, r 2.70(3).

(2) an address to which any payment which the managers or trustees are required to pay the party without pension rights is to be sent;
(3) if that address is a bank or building society or the Department of National Savings, sufficient details to enable payment to be made into that account.

After the order is made

The person in whose favour the order is made must serve it on the trustees or managers of the pension scheme. This applies also to orders amending or revoking earmarking orders. The spouse who is in receipt of an earmarking order needs to keep the pension scheme managers and trustees informed of changes of addresses and bank details (Divorce etc (Pensions) Regulations 1996). Where the details supplied earlier have ceased to have effect because the spouse with the order has remarried or for other reasons, the recipient of the earmarking order has to give notice to the trustees or managers of pension schemes within fourteen days of the event taking place.

Where it is not reasonably practicable for the pension scheme trustees to make the payment under the order because the details have not been given or kept up to date, the pension scheme must make the payment to the person with pension rights. The trustees are then discharged from their liability to make the payments under the order. The beneficiary is not able to recover payments from the scheme, but must attempt to claim them from the scheme member.

If the payments are made in error because the party without pension rights has failed to notify the pension scheme trustees or administrators of, for example, her remarriage, the pension scheme is absolved of liability if the payments were made in good faith and the pension scheme member will need to try to recover the payments made in error from the spouse.

Pension schemes must notify beneficiaries of transfers of pension benefits by the scheme member to another scheme and must give a copy of the order and details about payments to the new scheme. Schemes must also inform the beneficiaries of the earmarking order of any event likely to result in a significant reduction in the benefits payable under the scheme. These are not defined, but will include, for example, early retirement.

CONCLUSION

There are therefore some significant issues beginning to emerge in relation to the reforms.

First, and deeply problematical, is the sheer complexity and variety of the options now, or shortly to be, available. For solicitors and mediators to give advice to a client will involve high skills, including advising:

(1) whether set-off or earmarking is appropriate, and, if earmarking, whether a lump sum or periodical payments order is preferable;
(2) whether the CETV is satisfactory for either side, and evaluating whether and how a separate valuation (on the basis that the member will be staying in the scheme) should be commissioned, showing in particular the past service reserve or other information;
(3) whether the date of the valuation (about which the regulations are much exercised) is in fact relevant since a difference of a year or two is usually not material;
(4) whether a letter setting out the options to the client should be written, and if so how, since with hindsight many clients will find they have made the wrong decision, blame their adviser for not telling them about the downsides of their decision and seek redress;
(5) whether a letter to the client should be on file recording the advice that a spouse should write annually to the pension scheme with a note of the address; the regulations make it clear that it is not the scheme's job to keep track of the spouse, and, if they cannot find the spouse, they will pay the member instead;
(6) whether the fact that many clients will prefer the cash set-off at divorce, rather than an earmarking order, but will need to recognise that the cash will be reduced to take account of the fact it is tax-free, paid immediately rather than in the future, and is certain rather than contingent should be factored into the advice.

There are several other more strategic issues:

(7) whether the differing rules on contracting-out will in the end be material;
(8) whether the new choices of earmarking and sharing are sufficient, or whether derived rights should eventually be phased out in the European manner. Experience indicates that in the first two years that earmarking for example has been available fewer than 200 orders have been made by the courts;
(9) whether the tax structures underlying the pension system are sympathetic to the division of pension rights;
(10) whether pension rights are of such a nature that they do not lend themselves to satisfactory division, and other solutions should be found.[27]

---

27 There is a vast US literature on the position there; see, eg, Pension Benefit Guaranty Corporation, Divorce Orders and PBGC, PBGC, Washington DC, September 1996. This paper does not consider the practical issues to be faced by the administrators of pension schemes, and the position of employers who are less than comfortable in providing privatised social security protection much of which can be removed and given to someone not in contemplation of the employer.

Chapter 5

DIVIDING THE ASSETS ON BREAKDOWN OF RELATIONSHIPS OUTSIDE MARRIAGE: CHALLENGES FOR REFORMERS

Professor Rebecca Bailey-Harris

INTRODUCTION

What are the state's interests in regulating the financial consequences of the breakdown of relationships outside marriage? The following may be identified:

(a) the equalisation of the effects of the relationship on the parties' economic positions;
(b) the prevention of exploitation where there is or was a power imbalance;
(c) the recognition of pluralism in contemporary society;
(d) the removal of discrimination on the basis of marital status, gender or sexuality;
(e) the promotion of party autonomy;
(f) the clear definition of legal rights;
(g) the promotion of methods of dispute resolution which minimise conflicts and costs;
(h) the avoidance of an unjustified burden on the public purse.

There may be an unavoidable conflict between certain of these objectives,[1] in particular between (a) and (b) on the one hand and (c) and (e) on the other. In essence, that conflict represents the competing demands of paternalism and self-determination. Law-makers are ultimately faced with the choice between clashing social policies and cannot attempt to achieve a perfect reconciliation.

It is the writer's view that, in view of the manifest defects of the current law which will be examined shortly, and the consequent social injustice which is thereby perpetrated, this area should be given absolute priority in the government's agenda for family law reform.[2] Yet this has not proved to be the case: instead, ancillary relief has been singled out for urgent consideration (in the absence of clear evidence of public or professional discontent with the present system), and the Law Commission's discussion paper on the property rights of 'homesharers' remains long awaited.[3] The reason for the government's apparent unwillingness to grasp the nettle of financial consequences of

---

1   Bailey-Harris (1995) 9 *International Journal of Law and the Family* 233 at 334–336.
2   Others share this view: see, eg, Thorpe LJ supra Chapter 1, pp 8–9.
3   At the time of writing, the prediction for its release is Autumn 1998.

unmarried relationships is obscure, but it may reflect a continuing anxiety about 'family values' discourse which surfaced with dramatic results during the debates on the Family Homes and Domestic Violence Bill and the Family Law Bill in 1995 and 1996.

The policy debate on the direction of future reform is perhaps not assisted by any clear picture of the social context in which the current law operates in England and Wales. Cohabitation has undoubtedly risen in statistical popularity, but there are questions about the duration or permanency of relationships and in particular the number of heterosexuals who choose cohabitation as a real and long-term alternative to marriage, as opposed to a trial or precursor.[4] Cohabitants necessarily display more variety as a class than the married, since the former include homosexual as well as heterosexual couples; we shall see that the extent to which a single scheme of legal regulation should encompass both is one of the major policy issues which the law must resolve.

THE CURRENT LAW

The distribution of assets[5] between an unmarried couple on the breakdown of their relationship is governed primarily by the general law, with prominence in disputed cases involving owner-occupied property given to the equitable principles of trusts and proprietary estoppel, or by contract in the form of a cohabitation agreement where the parties have made one.[6] Statute plays a limited role; an example is the transfer of tenancies between heterosexual cohabitants under Part IV of the Family Law Act 1996.[7] The emphasis of the general law in relation to owner-occupied property is largely on the ascertainment of existing rights and not on the alteration of entitlements, in contrast to the exercise of the flexible discretion to bring about a fair outcome which characterises the division of assets between husband and wife on marriage breakdown.[8] Moreover there is no obligation to maintain an unmarried partner (as opposed to his or her children).[9] In principle there is nothing specific to family members about the application of common law and

---

4   See, eg, *The Family Lawyer's Handbook* Bailey-Harris (ed) (The Law Society, 1997), pp 144–145; Barlow *Cohabitants and the Law* (Butterworths, 1997), pp 6–7.
5   This chapter does not discuss the regulation of occupation in the home: see the Family Law Act 1996, ss 33 and 36.
6   For detailed discussion, see Cretney and Masson *Principles of Family Law* (6th edn) (Sweet & Maxwell, 1997), pp 116–118 and chapter 5; *The Family Lawyer's Handbook* Bailey-Harris (ed) (The Law Society, 1997), chapter 6; Barlow op cit note 4 supra, chapter 11.
7   The Trusts of Land and Appointment of Trustees Act 1996 applies to the regulation of disputes between equitable co-owners generally and is not specific in any way to particular family relationships: see Baughen 'Trusts of Land and Family Practice' [1996] Fam Law 736.
8   Matrimonial Causes Act 1973, Part II.
9   Under the Child Support Act 1996, the Matrimonial Causes Act 1973, Part II, and Sch 1 to the Children Act 1989.

equitable principles, although, as will be discussed later, in reality the characteristics of the particular relationship may colour the outcome.

STRENGTHS OF THE CURRENT LAW

One may be somewhat hard-pressed to identify the strengths of the current law, since the consistent focus of most commentators is on its shortcomings. Nevertheless the following may with some pains be extracted.

Formal neutrality as to family form, gender and sexuality

The relevant equitable doctrines are not confined in operation to particular categories of persons, but in principle apply neutrally across a wide range, which means that the law avoids judgments about the particular model of family relationship to be regulated. So, for instance, recent reported cases on constructive trusts and proprietary estoppel involve homosexual as well as heterosexual partners. Of the decision in *Wayling v Jones*[10] it has been observed that:

> 'Nothing in Balcombe LJ's leading judgment ... suggests that the court attached any significance to the homosexual nature of the relationship in determining whether Wayling's conduct had been detrimental.'[11]

Moreover, the operation of the general law is formally not only sexuality- but also gender-neutral, although whether this is true in practice is questionable and will be discussed further below.

Flexibility

The general law is inherently capable of developments unrestricted by the political and practical factors limiting the availability and efficacy of statutory change. A recent example of trust law's development (in the context of quantification of the beneficial interests) is *Midland Bank v Cooke*.[12]

Moral basis

The concept underpinning the equitable doctrines of resulting, constructive and implied trusts, and that of proprietary estoppel, is that of unconscionability: equity intervenes because it would be unconscionable to permit the legal owner to assert strict legal rights. However, as we shall see, the basis of equitable intervention is not unconscionability *simpliciter*. English courts have

---

10 [1995] 2 FLR 1029.
11 Lawson 'The Things We Do for Love: Detrimental Reliance in the Family Home' (1996) 16 *Legal Studies* 218 at 227.
12 [1995] 2 FLR 915. Note that this case involved a married couple. Commentators have generally seen the decision as representing a more liberal approach: see, eg, Wragg 'Constructive Trusts and the Unmarried Couple' [1996] Fam Law 298.

declined to develop a single coherent concept of unconscionability or unfairness as the basis for equitable intervention, and the basic concept has tended to become subsumed in the technicalities of the individual doctrines.[13]

Party autonomy

Whilst there is a dearth of contemporary case-law on cohabitation contracts, publications designed primarily for practitioners commonly assume their validity and give detailed guidance on drafting.[14] Such contracts (which may incorporate declarations of trust) permit unmarried partners to determine the financial consequences of the eventual breakdown of their relationship with a greater degree of autonomy than has to date been permitted to their married counterparts; pre-marital contracts have not been regarded as conclusive and a court exercising ancillary relief jurisdiction under Part II of the Matrimonial Causes Act 1973 will regard the existence of such a contract only as a relevant factor under s 25.[15] The rationale for this difference may however lie more in a laissez-faire attitude of the state towards unmarried relationships – manifesting itself in the absence of a statutory adjustive regime for their benefit – than in a conscious promotion of party autonomy. Moreover, at the time of writing the government is considering whether to put forward proposals to accord pre-marital agreements greater status,[16] and so the sky may change in the near future.

WEAKNESSES OF THE CURRENT LAW

The weaknesses of the current law are far more self-evident.

Complexity and uncertainty, resulting in lack of clarity and inaccessibility

A number of distinct equitable doctrines can currently be invoked in the argument of a claim, and even experienced practitioners and judges are not always wholly clear on the relationship between them. In *Drake v Whipp*[17] Peter Gibson LJ in the Court of Appeal was critical of the confusion which in his view had crept into the law between the concept of resulting trust and that of constructive trust; in this particular case the claim had been incorrectly characterised in the court below as one of resulting trust, thereby precluding

---

13   See Cretney and Masson op cit note 6 supra, pp 127–128.
14   See, eg, *The Family Lawyer's Handbook* Bailey-Harris (ed) (The Law Society, 1997), pp 145–156; Lush *Co-Habitation and Co-Ownership Precedents* (Family Law, 1994); Hatley 'Contractual Freedom Within the Family' (1998) *International Family Law* 39.
15   See Harcus 'Pre-Nuptial Agreements' [1997] Fam Law 669; *F v F (Ancillary Relief: Substantial Assets)* [1995] 2 FLR 45; *Beach v Beach* [1995] 2 FLR 160.
16   The Lord Chancellor in Spring 1998 referred the issue for urgent consideration by the Advisory Group on Ancillary Relief; see the discussion by Thorpe LJ, Chapter 1.
17   [1996] 1 FLR 826.

proper consideration of a wider range of contributions in the determination of the quantum of the parties' respective shares in the beneficial ownership.[18] Nor are academic commentators unanimous in the meanings to be attributed to the three terms 'resulting', 'implied' and 'constructive' trust; the conventional view is that the latter two are both founded on common intention, but Dr Cretney has warned of the 'dangers in indiscriminate use of the terminology of the constructive trust'.[19] A popular practitioner's handbook asserts that '... a number of key judgments blur the distinctions ... Some seem to create hybrids.'[20]

A further source of confusion is the relationship between the doctrine of proprietary estoppel and that of constructive trust; Glover and Todd argue that the decision in *Lloyds Bank v Rosset*[21] merges the two concepts.[22] This confusion is of far more than academic interest; it has obvious implications for access to justice. Uncertainty in the applicable doctrines and in their interrelationship means that in practice claims are expensive to litigate and the outcome is unpredictable. This may well deter parties from seeking to enforce their rights, particularly in a climate of ever-reducing public expenditure on legal aid.

Complex and uncertain law is accessible only to specialised experts and not to the ordinary citizen. Practitioners frequently comment on public misapprehensions as to the property rights of those in unmarried relationships; a common illusion is that there is a doctrine of 'common law marriage' in domestic law[23] which confers rights on breakdown equivalent to those attaching to marriage.[24] A primary goal of law reformers must unarguably be the clarification of the law so that such misconceptions are removed. Another concern must be to ensure that negotiated settlements adequately reflect legal rights, a particular challenge in the current climate of promotion of mediation against a background of reducing legal aid.

Particular areas of difficulty and uncertainty in the current law are: the nature of contributions which will give rise to an inference of a common intention that a beneficial interest is conferred under a constructive trust; the assessment of the quantum of a beneficial interest once one is established; and, under both the doctrines of constructive trust and proprietary estoppel, what is meant by detrimental reliance.

---

18 Glover and Todd argue that since *Gissing v Gissing* [1971] AC 886 the resulting and constructive trust have not been properly differentiated: 'The Myth of Common Intention' (1996) 16 *Legal Studies* 325 at 328.
19 Cretney and Masson op cit note 6 supra, p 138.
20 *The Family Lawyer's Handbook* op cit note 4 supra, p 165.
21 [1991] AC 107.
22 'The Myth of Common Intention' (1996) 16 *Legal Studies* 325 at 326, 327.
23 As opposed to the established doctrine in private international law.
24 Lawson-Cruttenden and Odutola 'Constructive Trusts – A Practical Guide' [1995] Fam Law 560–561; Wragg loc cit note 12 supra.

In *Lloyds Bank v Rosset* [25] Lord Bridge expounded what has now become the classic formulation of the two categories of condition for establishing a beneficial interest under a constructive or implied trust. In simple terms, these are either: (i) agreement as to beneficial ownership, evidenced by actual discussion, prior to purchase, plus the claimant acting to his or her detriment in reliance thereon; or (ii) where a common intention as to beneficial ownership may be inferred from the parties' conduct, requiring that the claimant made some direct contribution to the acquisition of the property, such contributions establishing also that the claimant has acted to his or her detriment. In *Rosset* Lord Bridge was 'extremely doubtful'[26] whether anything other than direct financial contributions to acquisition costs would give rise to the necessary inference of intention and detriment. Financial contributions to the expenses of a common lifestyle would thus appear to be excluded in principle, but the case-law is not entirely clear. In *Grant v Edwards*[27] the woman made substantial contributions to general household expenses while the man paid the deposit and the mortgage instalments on the house which was in his name. On appeal the court declared that she was entitled to a half-interest in the property. The rationale offered was that her contribution to general household expenses was in excess of what was normally to be expected and that without that substantial contribution the man would not have been able to keep up the mortgage payments. Nevertheless, such reasoning must necessarily be productive of fine distinctions . The situation is made even more complex (not to say illogical) by the decision in *Midland Bank v Cooke*,[28] which expounds a two-stage approach. First, if there is a direct contribution to the purchase, however small (in this case a sum equivalent to 6.5%), a beneficial interest will arise; secondly, in ascertaining the quantum of that beneficial interest, a wider range of contributions – apparently including general financial contributions to the common life and non-financial contributions to family welfare – may be taken into account by the court. In the result the quantum of the claimant's share was assessed at 50%. This decision has been criticised by some commentators[29] on the ground of its apparent inconsistency with the *Rosset* approach, and for its illogicality. Nevertheless the decision may be welcomed[30] on the pragmatic ground of achieving a more just outcome (at least in some cases where there is some direct contribution to the purchase) reflecting the reality of role-division within a cohabitation relationship. Be this as it may, it certainly does little to reduce uncertainty. Wragg has observed that:

---

25   [1991] AC 107.
26   Ibid, 133.
27   [1986] 3 WLR 114.
28   [1995] 2 FLR 915.
29   Palowski '*Midland Bank v Cooke* – A New Heresy?' [1996] Fam Law 484; Battersby 'How Not to Judge the Quantum (and Priority) of a Share in the Family Home' [1996] *Child and Family Law Quarterly* 261; *The Family Lawyer's Handbook* op cit note 4 supra, 172.
30   Lawson-Cruttenden and Odutola 'Constructive Trusts – A Practical Guide' [1995] Fam Law 560 at 563.

> 'In the circumstances, it may seem churlish to criticise any liberalisation of the law, however modest. It is submitted, however, that the nature of the liberalisation represented by the decision ... may, in practice, achieve little more than anomaly and uncertainty in an area already characterised by these features ... Tinkering with the problem by introducing new criteria into stage 2 [ie the assessment of the quantum of the beneficial interest] provides no real solution.'[31]

Cretney has highlighted the arbitrary operation of the decision:

> 'The view that different criteria apply to the threshold condition ... and to the question of quantifying that interest may seem somewhat artificial. It is certainly difficult to understand how a woman who has given 18 years of her life to caring for her partner, his home and their children should be entitled to nothing [*Burns v Burns*] whereas another (in all respects in identical circumstances, save that the partner's parents had paid £100 towards the deposit on a house) should be entitled to half the proceeds of sale.'[32]

A second particular problem is the notion of detrimental reliance, which is a necessary component of both the constructive trust and proprietary estoppel. Lawson has described the results arrived at in the decided cases as 'arbitrary and unrealistic'.[33] One issue is the nature of the detriment: to what extent must the conduct be referrable to the property in question? In *Rosset* the House of Lords held not only that the wife's contributions (supervision of building, interior decorating, arranging home security and insurance) were insufficient to give rise to an equitable interest, but also doubted whether such 'trifling contributions' amounted to detriment.[34] By contrast in *Grant v Edwards*[35] Browne-Wilkinson V-C (as he then was) went so far as to say that acts do not have to be inherently referrable to the property in question. Some commentators contrast the narrow judicial approach to the nature of contributions giving rise to an interest with the liberal approach to conduct relied on as detriment, and maintain that this contrasting approach is illogical and poses problems in practice.[36] The principal issue in *Wayling v Jones*,[37] a case on proprietary estoppel, was that of reliance: did the promise relied upon have to be the sole inducement for the plaintiff's conduct? It was held that it did not. A powerful criticism of the operation of the detrimental reliance requirement in the case-law is that it embodies 'stereotyped notions of behaviour'.[38] Thus it is difficult for a family member to establish detriment

---

31   'Constructive Trusts and the Unmarried Couple' [1996] Fam Law 298 at 300.
32   Cretney and Masson op cit note 13 supra, 146.
33   (1996) 16 *Legal Studies* 218 at 231.
34   [1991] AC 107 at 132–133.
35   [1987] 1 FLR 87 .
36   Lawson-Cruttenden and Odutola [1996] Fam Law 560 at 561–562
37   [1995] 2 FLR 1029.
38   Lawson 'The Things We Do For Love: Detrimental Reliance in the Family Home' (1996) 16 *Legal Studies* 218 at 219.

unless he or she does something extraordinary, anything less being regarded as done 'for love and affection'.[39] Equally objectionable is the potential (discussed below) of the concept of detrimental reliance to operate with conscious or unconscious gender-bias.

A third problem area is the quantification of the beneficial interests under a constructive trust. Outcomes were always difficult to predict with precision and the authorities were never easy to reconcile.[40] *Midland Bank v Cooke*[41] has done nothing to introduce greater predictability. Contrast the outcome of the woman's share in that case (50%) with that on seemingly similar facts in *Drake v Whipp*[42] (33%).[43]

Need to prove intention to create a constructive trust

The parties' common intention is, jurisprudentially, an essential basis of the constructive or implied trust in England.[44] Intention is a pure question of fact, necessarily giving rise to serious evidentiary problems in the context of dealings with family members over the course of a long relationship. In reality its ascertainment by the court can become a largely fictitious[45] exercise. Particular problems arise in relation to the search for actual agreement under the first test in *Lloyds Bank v Rosset*.[46] Waite J (as he then was) has encapsulated the essence of the problem with eloquence:

> '... the tenderest exchanges of a ... courtship may assume an unforseen significance many years later when they are brought under equity's microscope and subjected to an analysis under which many thousands of pounds of value may be liable to turn ...'[47]

In reality many couples do not think at all about the details of beneficial ownership, particularly at the start of a relationship. It is unfortunate that English law has not been prepared to embrace the notion of the remedial constructive trust, imposed on a party irrespective of his or her actual intention, to prevent unconscionable conduct. Such a trust, liberated from the

---

39   See the remarks of Lord Bridge in *Lloyds Bank v Rosset* [1991] AC 107 at 132–133, and contrast the outcome in *Grant v Edwards* [1987] 1 FLR 87.
40   Cretney and Masson op cit note 13 supra, 143.
41   [1995] 2 FLR 915.
42   [1996] 1 FLR 826.
43   See the Comment by Bailey-Harris in [1996] Fam Law 472.
44   *Pettitt v Pettitt* [1970] AC 777; *Gissing v Gissing* [1971] AC 886; *Lloyds Bank v Rosset* [1991] AC 107.
45   Some argue that the search for common intention is not only fictitious but misconceived: see, eg, Glover and Todd 'The Myth of Common Intention' (1996) 16 *Legal Studies* 325.
46   [1991] AC 107.
47   *H v M (Property: Beneficial Interest)* [1992] 1 FLR 229 at 242.

constraints and fictions of common intention, has become well established both in Australia[48] and Canada.[49]

Trust law gives inadequate recognition of non-financial contributions to the relationship

It should be more than apparent from the foregoing discussion that the doctrines of resulting and constructive trusts give inadequate recognition to non-financial contributions to family welfare. Even the decision in *Midland Bank v Cooke*[50] is of limited assistance in remedying the problem since it permits a wider range of contributions to be taken into account only at the second stage of quantifying the beneficial interest, and leaves without any interest in the first place a party who has made no contribution to the acquisition of property.[51] It is obvious therefore that the constructive trust continues to favour the wage-earning, property-acquiring role in a family relationship. This approach immediately disables the law from attaining the equalisation, on breakdown, of the economic effects of the relationship on the parties. The law simply does not recognise the diversity of arrangements made in personal relationships, nor the subtle blending of the parties' efforts. More than a quarter of a century ago, Lord Denning MR highlighted the inadequacies of traditional trusts doctrines in recognising the role of the homemaker and parent in determining entitlement to assets on breakdown of a relationship.[52] For married persons that defect was remedied by the enactment of the Matrimonial Proceedings and Property Act 1970, but the unmarried still await justice.

Law operates with gender-bias in practice

Despite its formal neutrality, there are several accusations of discrimination which may be levelled against the law in its practical operation. The first follows obviously from the point made immediately above: to undervalue non-financial contributions in the determination of beneficial interests will impact negatively and disproportionately on those who bear children and continue to bear the primary role for their care, ie women. Secondly, the law appears to make stereotyped assumptions about the roles assumed by women and men respectively. The case-law suggests that courts tend to regard certain contributions to the relationship as being made in the case of a woman for 'sheer affection' or 'because that is the sort of thing women do', whereas similar contributions made by a man are regarded as evidence of detriment and

---

48 *Muschinski v Dodds* (1985) 160 CLR 583; *Baumgartner v Baumgartner* (1987) 164 CLR 137. See Finlay, Bailey-Harris and Otlowski *Family Law in Australia* 5th edn (Butterworths, 1997), pp 317–325.
49 *Pettkus v Becker* (1980) 117 DLR (3d) 257.
50 [1995] 2 FLR 915.
51 See Cretney and Masson op cit note 13 supra, 146; Wragg [1996] Fam Law 298.
52 *Wachtel v Wachtel* [1973] Fam 72.

therefore as giving rise to an entitlement. Here one may contrast the outcomes in, for example, *Burns* and *Rosset* with that in *Wayling v Jones*. This argument has been persuasively advanced by a number of commentators.[53]

Inadequate consideration of future needs

Equity's primary focus is retrospective, asking what happened in the past, whether in terms of actual agreements or contributions from which intentions can be inferred. The equitable doctrines thus give inadequate considerations to prospective factors, in particular those economic consequences which have resulted from role-divisions undertaken during the relationship. This approach contrasts strongly with the factors relevant in the exercise of the ancillary relief jurisdiction on divorce,[54] and is reinforced by the absence of any statutory provision for the payment of maintenance to a former partner in his or her own right (as opposed to child support or maintenance or provision to the parent with care for the benefit of a child).[55] A suggested justification for exclusion of prospective consideration in the case of unmarried relationships is that such relationships – unlike marriage – are not intended to create life-long obligations. In the present writer's view, this is misconceived; prospective considerations should be relevant in either case. The aim of the law should be to equalise the economic effects which the relationship (through the roles assumed by the parties), and this must involve consideration of their future economic prospects.

Inadequate consideration of future resources and the 'new property'

The equitable doctrines discussed above operate on vested property or funds and largely take account only of existing entitlements. One may contrast the increasing powers of the courts in the exercise of the ancillary relief jurisdiction on the divorce of a married couple to take account of future financial resources, in particular, future pension entitlements, and to make a range of orders in relation thereto.[56] The rationale for such extended powers is that for many couples, future pension entitlements represent substantial future security and a real asset to which both have contributed. It is unfortunate that such assets are for the unmarried largely beyond the scope of remedies available under the current law.

---

53 See, eg, Lawson (1996) 16 *Legal Studies* 218, esp 226–228;
54 Matrimonial Causes Act 1973, ss 25–25D.
55 Child Support Act 1991; Children Act 1989, Sch 1.
56 Matrimonial Causes Act 1973, s 25(2)(a), (h), ss 25B–25D; Family Law Act 1996, s 16; White Paper 'Pension Rights on Divorce', Cm 3564 (1997); 'Pension Sharing on Divorce: Reforming Pensions for a Fairer Future' (DSS, June 1998).

CHALLENGES FOR THE DIRECTION OF FUTURE REFORMS

Assuming that the defects of the current law are sufficiently self-evident to make the case for reform unarguable, and moreover accepting that statute is the preferable vehicle for reform, there nevertheless remain difficult issues to be confronted by law-makers. The experience of countries overseas which have embarked upon a course of statutory reform shows that policy dilemmas continue to be a preoccupation, and that some hard choices between competing interests have to be made.[57] Moreover, the direction of future reform is likely to be determined not only by choices of social policy but also by political practicalities, including (it is submitted, regrettably) the strength of 'family values' discourse.

Party autonomy versus state paternalism

A fundamental choice has inevitably to be made between the competing interests of party autonomy and state paternalism/maternalism in the regulation of the economic consequences of the breakdown of relationships outside marriage. This classic dilemma between different values was highlighted at the outset of this chapter. It finds one expression in the competing models of an adjustive regime imposed on defined relationships by operation of law, and an 'opt-in' system of registered partnership exemplified by Danish law.[58] The present writer is an avowed legal maternalist[59] and so favours the imposition of an adjustive regime. An 'opt-in' model which makes legal protection dependent on the consent of both parties to registration provides no adequate safeguard to the position of the more vulnerable and less empowered party. Moreover, the values expressed in a legislative regime of general application may have an educative effect on society, for instance as to the values to be accorded to the parties' different roles within a relationship.

Should the content of the law differ from or mirror that applying on marriage breakdown?

This deceptively simple question is merely the symptom of more profound ones. The autonomy/paternalism debate resurfaces here: should a couple be free to choose a family form with consequences distinct from the very institution (marriage) which they have consciously rejected? Is a society which purports to promote pluralism obliged to promote a range of real alternatives

---

57   On the Australian experience in particular, see Finlay, Bailey-Harris and Otlowski op cit note 48 supra, 313–345.

58   Broberg 'The Registered Partnership for Same-Sex Couples in Denmark' [1996] *Child and Family Law Quarterly* 149; Anderson 'Registered Personal Partnerships' [1997] Fam Law 174.

59   Bailey-Harris 'Law and the Unmarried Couple: Oppression or Liberation?' [1996] *Child and Family Law Quarterly* 137 at 140.

in family forms, all with different consequences? To do otherwise arguably reduces choice to 'Marriage Mark I' and 'Marriage Mark II', and renders its substance illusory. This is a difficult issue which does not admit of a ready reconciliation of competing social policies. Less problematical, in the writer's view, is to meet the argument (prevalent in 'family values' discourse) that the assimilation of the consequences of married and unmarried relationships undermines marriage.

The solution lies in the identification of the dominant values amongst the state's legitimate interests in the regulation of family breakdown, which have been outlined at the start of this chapter. The identification process necessitates an unavoidable choice between competing social policies. The writer's view is that the state should give priority to the aims of equalising the economic effect of relationship breakdown, and to the prevention of exploitation.[60] Given that function, the goal of removal of discrimination can also be achieved. The aim of the law governing asset distribution on the breakdown of *any* couple's relationship should be to make a fair allowance for the economic effects of the roles the parties have adopted, ie for the subtle blending of their efforts during their time together. This aim is neutral both as to the status of the relationship and the sexuality of the parties[61] (a view shared by some other writers[62] although not by all).[63] This approach supports an assimilation of the substance of the law between the married and the unmarried in this particular context, but with the retention of a sufficient width of discretion to permit the outcome to be tailored to meet the particular needs of the particular relationship, thereby also satisfying the claims of diversity and pluralism.

The definition of the relationship

Policy-makers and drafters alike must confront the important issue of defining the relationships outside marriage to which the operation of an adjustive regime is to be attached. Those states and territories in Australia which have undertaken the process of statutory reform have – with one exception – all opted for the 'cohabitation model': an unmarried version of the *consortium vitae*, confined to the heterosexual couple.[64] Only the Australian Capital Territory has opted for a different approach, identifying a 'domestic relationship' which does not depend on sexuality or even cohabitation.[65] Another

---

60 'Financial Rights in Relationships Outside Marriage' (1995) 9 *International Journal of Law and the Family* 233 at 234–237; [1996] *Child and Family Law Quarterly* 137 at 140–143. *Family Law in Australia* op cit note 48 supra, 313–316.
61 Bailey-Harris 'Property Disputes In De Facto Relationships' in *Equity: Issues and Trends* Cope (ed) (Federation Press, 1995) 181, 201–203.
62 Chisholm, Jessep and O'Ryan (1991) 5 *Australian Journal of Family Law* 241, 264, 266.
63 See, eg, Neave in *Equity: Issues and Trends* op cit note 61 supra, 219–225
64 New South Wales, Victoria, the Northern Territory, South Australia: see Finlay, Bailey-Harris and Otlowski op cit note 48 supra, 326–328.
65 Domestic Relationships Act 1994 (ACT), s 3(1).

definitional issue is whether indicators of stability are appropriate, and, if so, what they should be.

The writer's own view of the appropriate definition follows inevitably from her conception of the law's role described above. A law which aims for the fair adjustment between the parties of the economic effects of their common life can be broad in its definition of the relevant relationship; it is the *effects* of the relationship, rather than its classification, which are important. There are many possible indicators of mutual commitment in a relationship, and the law should accordingly adopt a broad definition. Certainly the statutory formulation should be sexuality-neutral. Arguably there is no need to make sexual relations a necessary component, since this element may not in reality be a component of the shared life. Possible models which break away from the more traditional cohabitation model of definition include those of 'domestic relationship' adopted in the Australian Capital Territory, and closer to home, 'associated persons' in Part IV of the Family Law Act 1996.[66] Indicators of commitment are in principle justified, in order to exclude casual or very short-lived relationships; a minimum duration of two years, with the alternative of the birth of a child, would be appropriate and have been utilised in the legislative models in Australia.[67]

The content of reformed principles of asset distribution

This chapter advocates the enactment of an adjustive regime to govern asset distribution on the breakdown of relationships outside marriage; the next fundamental question is necessarily the formulation of detailed principles. These – as is the case with the definition of relationship – will flow from the nature of the law's role which has been identified above.

Given the obligation to do justice to a diverse range of relationships, it follows that an adjustive statutory regime must embody a substantial element of discretion. The statute must contain a wide range of relevant considerations, whose application to the facts of a particular case must be a matter for judicial discretion. Whilst this model will necessarily involve a degree of unpredictability in outcome, nothing else will ensure that the outcome can be tailored to meet the particular circumstances of the particular relationship. It was noted at the outset of this chapter that the range of variety in unmarried relationships is greater than that in marriage. A further question is whether the exercise of discretion should be structured by the articulation, on the face of the statute, of express objectives; an example would be that of the equalisation of the economic effects of the relationship. The substance of the statute must also

---

66 Family Law Act 1996, s 62(3).
67 See Finlay, Bailey-Harris and Otlowski op cit note 48 supra, 326.

address what are conveniently termed the 'contribution issue' and the 'equity issue'.[68] The former requires consideration of the desirability of incorporating a rebuttable presumption or starting point of equal division of assets, arguably to reflect recognition of the presumptive equal value of different contributions to a shared endeavour and the impossibility of the precise quantification of efforts which have been blended in a subtle way during the course of the relationship. This is currently under consideration in the context of possible reforms of the ancillary relief jurisdiction under Part II of the Matrimonial Causes Act 1973.[69] It would be most unfortunate if the process of law reform in each field were to be considered and conducted in isolation one from the other. If the principles of ancillary relief were to be amended to introduce a presumption of equal division of assets, and an adjustive regime to be attached to the breakdown of unmarried relationships which was founded on a far wider discretion, this should be as a result of conscious choice of social policy, and should not be the chance outcome of a piecemeal approach to family law reform.

The 'equity issue' looks to the objective of equalising the economic effects which the relationship has had on the parties' respective financial positions. To achieve this, the adjustive regime must include prospective considerations amongst those factors relevant to the distribution of both property and income; moreover there should be no draconic time-limit placed on periodic awards. A new statute in this country should decline to follow the model adopted in a majority of the Australian statutes, which have tended to confine the considerations relevant to property distribution between the unmarried to past contributions, and to adopt a short-term rehabilitative approach to periodic support.[70] The equalisation of the economic effects of a relationship should be seen as a legitimate right rather than as an indication of dependency, and this argument holds good just as much in relation to informal as to formal relationships.[71]

Finally, statutory reform must tackle the validity of cohabitation contracts, which cannot be left to languish *sub silentio* and should be seen as an integral part of the overall issue of financial adjustment. The scope to be accorded to such contracts against the background of the creation of a general adjustive regime raises once again the autonomy/paternalism debate. To what extent is the principle of self-determination (the parties' freedom to opt out) to be

---

68 See (in the context of financial adjustment on marriage breakdown) Eekelaar and Maclean 'Property and Financial Adjustment after Divorce in the 1990s – Unfinished Business' in *The Human Face of Law* Hawkins (ed) (Oxford, Clarendon Press, 1997), 225 at 230–240.
69 See the discussion by Thorpe LJ in Chapter 1, supra.
70 See Finlay, Bailey-Harris and Otlowski op cit note 48 supra, 328–337. The recent decision of the New South Wales Court of Appeal in *Evans v Marmont* (1997) 21 Fam LR 760 reaffirms the distinction in approach between married and unmarried relationships.
71 For this argument in relation to the financial consequences of divorce, see Bailey-Harris 'The Role of Maintenance and Property Orders in Redressing Inequality' (1998) 12 *Australian Journal of Family Law* 3–18.

circumscribed by safeguards designed to prevent exploitation and hardship, particularly in relation to the more vulnerable party where there is power imbalance? Safeguards should be built in both at the stage of formation (such as certification of independent legal advice) and at a later stage (for instance, the court's power to vary terms where significantly changed circumstances require). Special provisions will be necessary to protect children. However, safeguards must not be so extensive or intrusive as to deter couples from entering into contracts at all: it is once again necessary to strike a sensitive balance between competing social values. The statutory regimes in Australia show subtly differing responses to this particular dilemma[72] and the issue merits careful consideration by policy-makers in England. The writer's own view is that the dominant values here (as in relation to the substance of the general regime) are the fair adjustment of the economic consequences of a relationship and the prevention of exploitation, to which that of party autonomy must ultimately yield.

---

72 Finlay, Bailey-Harris and Otlowski op cit note 48 supra, 345–348; Bailey-Harris (1995) *International Journal of Law and the Family* 233 at 249.

Chapter 6

ASSET DISTRIBUTION AFTER UNMARRIED COHABITATION: A UNITED STATES PERSPECTIVE

Professor Frances Olsen[1]

INTRODUCTION

There is an old saying I recently made up: 'Today's radical demand becomes tomorrow's conservative prop.' A related saying would be: 'Today's conservative prop may have been yesterday's radical innovation.' So it has been with the legal treatment of unmarried cohabitation (or 'nonmarital cohabitation' as it is generally referred to in the United States).

With the growing demand by same-sex couples for the right to marry (a demand that began as a kind of oddity a few years ago, opposed by many in the gay community) and its wide acceptance by progressive thinkers and even by the Supreme Court of Hawaii,[2] some conservatives have begun to support granting a degree of legal recognition to couples living together without being married to one another. It should be understood that 'conservative' is here used as a relative term; America is teeming with fundamentalist Christians who lay claim to the term 'conservative' and continue to find a case such as *Marvin v Marvin*[3] a sinful abomination. Moreover, those conservatives who do support

---

[1] Overseas Fellow, Churchill College, Cambridge University and Professor of Law, University of California at Los Angeles (UCLA). For her energy, good nature and scholarly work, I would like to thank Professor Rebecca Bailey-Harris, my meeting with whom was one of the many pleasant and valuable ripples to come out of Philip Alston's conference on the United Nations Convention on the Rights of the Child, held at Australian National University, Canberra, Australia. I also thank Professor Michael Freeman for coming to the SPTL conference held at King's College, London, and for his most helpful comments at the conference. Financial support for this essay was supplied by a Summer Grant from the UCLA Dean's Fund, for which I express my gratitude. I offer special thanks to the UCLA Law Library, and especially Linda Karr O'Connor, for valuable research assistance.

[2] *Baehr v Lewin* 74 Haw 530; 852 P 2d 44 (1993).

[3] 18 Cal 3d 660; 557 P 2d 106; 134 Cal Rptr 815 (1976); discussed further infra.

Marvin support it in a qualified manner, as a kind of lesser evil. Yet, in Hawaii[4] and in many political debates throughout the United States,[5] one sees a linkage between provisions barring same-sex marriage and provisions granting many – but importantly not all – of the benefits of marriage to unmarried couples who declare themselves to be or appear to be in a committed long-term relationship.

When the case of *Marvin v Marvin* was decided, it was considered by many to be a wildly innovative endorsement of sexual liberation, a 'classic California case'. Because it involved the movie star Lee Marvin, some saw it as coming straight out of Hollywood, steeped in Hollywood morals – or lack of morals. Of course, what the *Marvin* case actually did was to impose a degree of financial responsibility on the wealthier partner to unmarried cohabitation – hardly a policy designed to encourage lascivious abandonment. *Marvin* held that an unmarried cohabitant[6] ending a relationship could seek judicial enforcement of express or implied contracts with his or her cohabitant as well as seek *quantum meruit* or equitable remedies such as constructive or resulting trusts.

Protection for parties living in unmarried cohabitation, which seemed revolutionary to many in the 1970s, has come to be used as a conservative prop to the demand that marriage be reserved for those of the 'opposite' sex. Thus, this would seem to be a good time to take a fresh look at the law of unmarried cohabitation. The focus of this chapter will be the financial recovery allowed by one cohabitant against the other.

I. A DIVERSITY OF APPROACHES

As each of the 50 States in the United States is entitled to create its own family law regime, within limits set by the United States Constitution and by certain, very limited, federal laws, it is no surprise that there are a variety of laws dealing with unmarried cohabitation in the different American jurisdictions.

---

4   After the Hawaii Supreme Court remanded the *Baehr* case for trial to determine whether the state could show a compelling interest in barring same-sex couples from marrying, the trial court ruled in favour of the same-sex couple; the court allowed a stay pending appeal and as this book goes to press the Hawaii Supreme Court has not yet issued its final ruling. Meanwhile, the legislature has enacted legislation granting financial rights similar to those enjoyed by married people to a wide variety of unmarried people who cannot marry one another (for whatever reason), and has begun the process of amending the Hawaii constitution to empower the legislature to forbid same-sex marriage without interference from the courts. See Jonathan Goldberg-Hiller 'The Status of Status: Reciprocal Beneficiaries, Domestic Partnership, and Alternatives to Same-sex Marriage', paper delivered to the Gender, Sexuality and Law Conference, Keele University, 19–21 June 1998.
5   Congressional efforts to back various forms of domestic partner protection on to the Defense of Marriage Act, Pub L 104–199 (Sept. 21, 1996) were unsuccessful, however.
6   The term 'unmarried cohabitant', as it has been used, means a person who is not legally married to the person with whom he or she is living. Being married to someone else is generally treated as irrelevant.

The laws can be divided into four categories: those that follow the 'traditional' approach of denying recovery; those that grant recovery under written contracts only; those that allow legal enforcement of most contracts, written or unwritten, and express or implied in fact; and those generally following *Marvin* in both enforcing contracts between unmarried cohabitants and allowing for various equitable remedies.

A. The 'traditional' approach of Illinois

The most notorious jurisdiction in the United States on the issue of unmarried cohabitation is Illinois, a State in the American midwest whose politics have been dominated by down-State, rural citizens, despite the fact that the large city of Chicago is in the northeast corner of the State. Illinois established this dubious distinction in 1979, when its State Supreme Court decided the case of *Hewitt v Hewitt*.[7]

Hewitt involved a couple who had lived together as husband and wife for 15 years and had three children. They had apparently told virtually everyone that they were married, although in fact they were not. When the relationship broke down, the woman sued for divorce; the man opposed divorce on the basis that there was no marriage to dissolve and claimed the right to keep all the property, which was in his name. While acknowledging a responsibility to the children, he denied any financial responsibility to their mother, who had been his domestic companion for 15 years, had helped him through graduate school and contributed in other ways to the high earning capacity with which he left the relationship.

The plaintiff amended her complaint to ask for contractual and equitable remedies based on the period of cohabitation, and when the trial court dismissed her complaint, appealed. The intermediate court of appeals ruled that the woman had a cause of action based on her allegations of an express oral contract, noting that the couple had lived 'a most conventional, respectable and ordinary family life'.[8] The Illinois Supreme Court overturned the decision and specifically rejected the *Marvin* precedent. The Court cited an 1882 case[9] and bragged that 'Illinois' public policy ... was implemented long ago'.[10] It also expressed doubt whether 'the increasing numbers of unmarried cohabitants and the changing mores of our society ... reached the point at which the general welfare of the citizens of this State is best served by a return to something resembling the judicially created common law marriage our legislature outlawed in 1905'.[11]

---

7 77 Ill 2d 49; 394 NE 2d 1204 (1979). See also *Rehak v Mathia* 238 SE 2d 81 (Ga 1977).
8 *Hewitt v Hewitt*, 62 Ill App 3d 861, 863, 20 Ill Dec 476, 478, 380 NE 2d 454, 457, quoted in *Hewitt v Hewitt*, 77 Ill 2d 49, 54, 394 NE 2d 1204, 1206 (1979).
9 *Wallace v Rappleye*, 103 Ill 229, 249 (1882) ('An agreement in consideration of future illicit cohabitation between the plaintiffs is void').
10 77 Ill at 58–59, 394 NE 2d at 1208.
11 Ibid at 58, 394 NE 2d at 1208.

It may be useful at this point to distinguish two kinds of cases:

(1) cases in which the plaintiff's claim might be said to depend upon the cohabitation; and
(2) cases in which the plaintiff would have a good claim but for the fact of cohabitation.

Cases of the first category might include equitable claims based upon unpaid domestic work done under circumstances in which the value of the work would not ordinarily be recoverable and cases in which any recovery would be based upon considerations of justice within the particular relationship. Cases of the second kind include cases in which the parties clearly acted as business partners and cases involving an express agreement that would be enforceable under ordinary contractual principles.

It might seem difficult for courts to justify a refusal to enforce contracts that would ordinarily be valid, simply because the parties to the contract happened to be living together without being married. Here one could fairly say that one party to the contract is relying on the relationship to get out of his or her otherwise enforceable agreement, which would seem to be a direct benefit accruing to that party from the illicit cohabitation. The Illinois court relied in part on a slippery slope argument:[12] there are several points between which one cannot easily draw a line. Once express contracts are enforceable, what justification is there for refusing to enforce implied contracts? If implied-in-fact contracts are enforceable, how could one justify not enforcing implied-in-law contracts and allowing recovery in *quantum meruit* or forms of equitable remedies such as constructive or resulting trusts? Thus the Illinois court concluded that it should refuse to enforce any contracts between unmarried cohabitants.

An additional basis upon which Illinois refuses to enforce express contracts between unmarried cohabitants is its claim that realistically any such contract would involve illegal consideration – illicit sexual intercourse. The *Hewitt* decision referred to the:

> '... naiveté ... involved in the assertion that there are involved in these relationships contracts separate and independent from the sexual activity, and the assumption that those contracts would have been entered into or would continue without that activity.'[13]

---

12 Ibid at 57, 394 NE 2d at 1207.
13 Ibid at 60; 394 NE 2d at 1209.

Yet even in Illinois one can find the odd middle-level appellate case allowing recovery, for example to a woman who paid most of the cost of motor vehicles which were titled in the name of her cohabitant.[14]

The Illinois Supreme Court also expressed concern whether granting legal rights 'closely resembling' those of marriage would 'encourage the formation of [illicit] relationships and weaken marriage as the foundation of our family-based society'.[15] 'We cannot confidently say that judicial recognition of property rights between unmarried cohabitants will not make that alternative to marriage more attractive by allowing the parties to engage in such relationships with greater security.'[16]

The standard complaint levelled against these cases is that they are irrational in that they penalise parties for behaviour that is no longer socially unacceptable, or they penalise only one party to the cohabitation. What is often omitted is the recognition that they penalise the financially less well off, almost always the woman, and actually reward the man. Moreover, the underlying assumption motivating the court, perhaps unconsciously, seems to be the classic double standard of sexual morality. The court's assertions make sense mainly if one has a view of the world that women seek marriage and give sex in exchange for marriage, while men consent to marriage if a woman insists on it. A court's draconian refusal to distribute assets after unmarried cohabitation could be understood as a means to pressure the woman to insist on getting married.

This assumption of the double sexual standard is made more explicit in cases from the State of Louisiana. There, cohabitation is referred to as 'concubinage' and the terms used for unmarried cohabitants are gender specific. The woman is a 'concubine' and the man a 'paramour'.[17] As *Schwegmann v Schwegmann*[18] put it in a decision refusing to uphold an asserted contract and denying a woman any recovery:

> 'To equate the non-marital relationship of concubinage to a marital relationship is to do violence to the very structure of our civilized society. Without the family, the State cannot exist and without marriage the family cannot exist. Thus, aside from religious or moralistic values, the State is justified in encouraging the

---

14 See *Spafford v Coats*, 118 Ill App 3d 566, 455 NE 2d 241 (1983). One can also find the odd California case invalidating an alleged contract for illegal consideration when the agreement by one party to perform sexual 'services' was explicitly mentioned in the pleadings, *Jones v Daly*, 176 Cal Rptr 130 (1981). But see *Whorton v Dillingham*, 248 Cal Rptr 405, 409–10 (1988) (enforcing contract when allegation was of mutual sexual promises, found by court to be 'independent of the bargained for consideration').
15 77 Ill 2d at 58, 394 NE 2d at 1207.
16 Ibid at 61–62, 394 NE 2d at 1209.
17 See 29 *Idaho Law Rev* 975, 998 note 72. The concubine just 'lies' (cubare) whilst the paramour 'loves' (par amor, 'bylore').
18 441 So 2d 316 at 326 (La Ct App 1983).

legitimate (marriage) over the illegitimate (concubinage), for to do otherwise is to spread the seeds of destruction of the civilized society.'[19]

In an earlier case[20] the Louisiana Supreme Court refused to allow a woman any interest in a business she and her unmarried cohabitant operated, finding that the underlying purpose of the relationship was concubinage. Women must use their sex to get marriage; if their sexuality might have played any role or had anything to do with any property or money relations, they must be denied recovery.

B. The partial apparent reform of Minnesota

One state, by legislation, provides that contracts between unmarried cohabitants will be enforceable only if they are in writing. Minnesota's statute allows for the validity of an express written contract 'between a man and a woman who are living together ... out of wedlock' even if 'sexual relations between the parties are contemplated' but provides also that in the absence of such written contract, any claim to the earnings or property of another 'based on the fact that the individuals lived together in contemplation of sexual relations and out of wedlock' is contrary to public policy.[21]

While cohabitation contracts could be drafted to protect the financial interests of the party earning less money or acquiring fewer assets in her or his name, the more common practice is a contract doing the opposite and protecting the wealthier party from claims of the partner earning less money. The following example of a contract clearly drafted to provide protection to the financially better off party would nevertheless probably be enforceable:

> We have decided to begin living together on _____ . We do not intend that any common law marriage should arise from this. We have not made any promises to each other about economic matters. We do not intend any economic rights to arise from our relationship. If in the future we decide that any promises of an economic nature should exist between us, we will put them in writing, and only such written promises made by us in a written memorandum signed by us in the future shall have any force between us. Signed at _____ on _____ .[22]

While such a contract might initially seem fair enough to many couples if they are both working for pay, and especially if they earn approximately the same salary, over time it could become quite unfair. Like antenuptial agreements, a cohabitation agreement such as this may come to be unconscionable as circumstances change. If, for example, the man and woman have children and slip into a traditional division of labour, assets they accumulate are likely to be

---

19 441 So 2d at 326.
20 *Sparrow v Sparrow* 93 So 2d 232 (La 1957).
21 Minn Stat Ann 513.075, 076 (West 1990).
22 By William P Cantwell, quoted in Lawrence W Waggoner 'Marital Property Rights in Transition' 59 *Missouri Law Review* 21, 68 note 115 (1994).

in the man's name. Moreover, the man's earning capacity is likely to increase, as the family centres its activity to maximise his earnings, while the woman's earning capacity is likely to remain stagnant or decrease. When one party to the relationship obtains assets and an increased earning capacity at the expense of his or her partner, a contract keeping their property separate can be unconscionable, whether the couple was married or remained unmarried.

Most cohabitants at the present time do not sign any such contract. However much the financially advantaged party might appreciate the protection of such an agreement, many people contemplating cohabitation with someone of less economic means might be reluctant to broach the subject. Certainly the production of such a contract might discourage a person from entering into cohabitation, even if the person had had no intention of profiting financially from the cohabitation or could not imagine ever suing in the event that living together did not work out. Such a contract would serve as a reminder of the practicalities of life and as a potential damper on romantic illusions. It is not clear what effect it would have on the couple's decision to live together if the wealthier member were to propose such a contract explicitly limiting his (or her) financial liability. Perhaps some couples would change their mind.

It is also possible, that having signed such a contract, the economically weaker party would think to propose a revision of the contract if and when circumstances change making the contract manifestly unfair, for example when she (or he) relocates to another city to facilitate the other party's promotion or quits her (or his) job to take care of children born into the relationship. When the couple's financial situation changes, it might or might not occur to either of them to revise the contract.

It should be noted that the Minnesota law is likely to lead to greater injustice than this contract. In essence, the Minnesota law has the effect of treating unmarried cohabitants as though they had signed the contract quoted above. Yet, because they never actually signed such a contract, the couple is even less likely to prepare a written contract as their situation changes and the terms would become increasingly unfair. Insofar as the Minnesota law may appear superficially to carry out the intent of the parties, it would seem more liberal and less steeped in the double standard of sexual morality than the Illinois approach. Yet, in most cases, the Minnesota approach is just as likely to result in injustice.

C. Enforcing actual agreements only[23]

A third set of States enforce express contracts as long as they are not based on sexual services as consideration, whether or not the parties are living together without being married, but refuse to provide any general equitable remedy in the absence of an express contract.

---

23   No particular State is strongly associated with this position.

Often the stated basis for such a refusal to provide any greater remedy is that 'recovery based on principles of contracts implied in law essentially would resurrect the old common law marriage doctrine' specifically abolished by many State legislatures.[24] A variety of policies have served to protect unmarried parties to a domestic arrangement: common law marriage, putative spouse, presumption of marriage, estoppel and so forth. In recent years, only 13 of the 50 States, plus the District of Columbia, have provided for common law marriage to result from open cohabitation with intent to be married. All other States, however, would be expected to recognise the validity for all purposes of a common law marriage entered in one of these 14 jurisdictions.[25]

After the legislatures have enacted legislation to abolish common law marriage, some State courts have continued to use common law marriage ideas to validate relationships or justify financial judgments in favour of unmarried women. For example, in *Thomson v Thomson*,[26] the court upheld what appears to have been a common law marriage, years after the legislature in 1921 abolished the doctrine. The court concluded that 'a marriage may be circumstantially established by the fact that a man and a woman have for a considerable period of time openly cohabited as husband and wife and recognised and treated each other as such, so that they are generally reputed to be married among those who have come in contact with them'.[27] The court looked to the same factors that used to be evidence to establish a common law marriage and treated the factors as evidence of a valid ceremonial marriage. Again, in *Kellard v Kellard*,[28] a New York court took into consideration the parties' lengthy cohabitation purporting to be husband and wife in New York, after the state had abolished common law marriage, to determine that they were legally married even though they never went through a marriage ceremony. On vacation, the couple had spent one night together as husband and wife in South Carolina and two in Georgia, both of which States recognised common law marriage. Thus, the court asserted the parties had been married under the common law of South Carolina or Georgia or both, and this common law marriage should be recognised in New York.

The seeming resistance of courts to legislative efforts to abolish common law marriage results from the attempt of courts to avoid injustice between the parties in the individual case before the court. Abolishing common law

---

24 *Carnes v Sheldon* 311 NW 2d 747 (Mich Ct App, 1981).
25 A couple married under the common law would not cease to be husband and wife when they moved to a non-common law marriage State. The situation is more complicated, however, if a couple resident in a non-common law State purports to travel to a common law State and contract a marriage. Despite the requirements of the full faith and credit clause of the US Constitution, some States refuse to recognise efforts by their own domiciliaries to marry under the common law of a neighbouring state. See Nadine E Roddy *Interstate Recognition of Common Law Marriages* 4 Divorce Litig 77 (April, 1992).
26 236 Mo App 1223; 163 SW 2d 792 (1942).
27 236 Mo App 1231; 163 SW 2d 796.
28 13 Fam L Rep (BNA) 1490 (NY Sup Ct 1987).

marriage does not necessarily represent any public policy against protecting the financial interests of a person living with someone to whom she or he is not married. Courts refusing to enforce implied contracts do express concern with the 'sanctity of marriage', which they suggest has often played some role in the abolition of common law marriage, but the legislatures were always also influenced by many other factors. While some of the objections to common law marriage apply also to unmarried cohabitation, others do not. One concern is that the doctrine of common law marriage may encourage fraud and perjury, with a couple choosing to remain unmarried and then one or both parties falsely claiming to have had an intent to be married when this would serve the interests of one or both parties. This concern plays a role, though perhaps a lesser one, in deciding the financial treatment of unmarried cohabitation: one party might commit perjury to try to defraud the other, and in the case of oral contracts neither party may know just what the truth is, much less testify honestly. A more significant concern with common law marriage, not present with judicial recognition of unmarried cohabitation, is that common law marriage, combined with laws against bigamy, can invalidate subsequent marriages. A person who enters into a formal marriage in good faith may have no idea that his or her partner had a prior existing common law marriage; even the partner who entered into the common law marriage may be unaware that it constitutes an impediment and that the ceremonial marriage is bigamous and void. When an apparently valid marriage is declared bigamous on the basis of a preexisting common law marriage, it may result in unfair treatment of the people involved, and the possibility of some previous period of cohabitation being taken as constituting a common law marriage leads to significant uncertainty of marital status.

D. The *Marvin* approach of California

The California position goes perhaps the furthest in allowing a variety of equitable remedies and recognising the monetary value of unpaid domestic work. The general consensus would be that *Marvin* broke important new ground, leading the way to progressive reform in the Unites States (and eventually much of the world). In fact, however, *Marvin v Marvin* was not particularly revolutionary or unusual in terms of legal doctrine. A long string of cases from a variety of states granted financial remedies to one cohabitant against another before the *Marvin* case.[29] For example, cases from a variety of different States have found life partners, whether married or not, to be business

---

29 See, eg, *Latham v Latham*, 274 Or 421, 547 P 2d 144 (1976) (upholding express oral contract between unmarried cohabitants); *Greer v Richmond*, 369 Mass 47, 337 NE 2d 691 (1975) (granting surviving cohabitant *quantum meruit* recovery against estate of deceased partner); *Tyranski v Piggins*, 44 Mich App 570, 205 NW 2d 595 (1973) (enforcing express oral contract against estate of deceased cohabitant).

partners when they both contributed to a family business. *Chaachou v Chaachou*,[30] a 1961 case from Florida, found a common law marriage but clearly would have found a partnership between husband and wife otherwise.

Although the facts of *Marvin* are well known, it may be useful to repeat some of them. The plaintiff was a woman who had lived together with a movie star, Lee Marvin, for more than five years during and after the period in which he was leaving his first wife. When he became dissatisfied with the relationship and eventually threw out his unmarried cohabitant, she sued him for breach of alleged express contracts that: (1) they would pool their financial resources; and (2) that he would take care of her for the rest of her life. The trial court dismissed her complaint without trial and she appealed. The Supreme Court of California reversed, holding that express contracts between unmarried cohabitants are legally enforceable and that the plaintiff thus stated a good cause of action for trial. The California Supreme Court also went further, and suggested that if the facts developed at trial warranted it, there should be further remedies available, based on an implied contract, partnership, joint venture or other tacit understanding, *quantum meruit*, or constructive or resulting trusts.

The trial was sordid by 1970s standards, involving adultery, allegations of homosexuality, drunkenness, and 'pillow talk' promises.[31] To the surprise of few, the woman was found unable to establish her claim under any of the generous provisions suggested by the Supreme Court. The trial court forged an additional remedy, referred to by commentators as 'palimony',[32] to provide to sexual 'pals' some of the kinds of rehabilitative relief that courts at that time were increasingly giving to divorcing wives as 'temporary' alimony, as an alternative to enforcing any ongoing duty of support. This novel effort at generosity by the trial judge who had disbelieved the factual claims of the woman was overturned by the Court of Appeal,[33] leaving the woman with nothing except the publicity and distinction of a starring role in a major American family law decision.

Marvin was touted as a major breakthrough toward the social acceptance of unmarried cohabitation. Indeed, the Court did comment upon the growing incidence of such living arrangements:

> '[T]he prevalence of nonmarital relationships in modern society and the social acceptance of them, marks this as a time when our courts should by no means apply the doctrine of unlawfulness of the so-called meretricious relationship to the instant case.... The mores of society have indeed changed so radically in regard to

---

30 135 So 2d 206 (Fla 1961).
31 See *Marvin v Marvin*, 5 Mam L Rep 3077 (Super Ct of Calif 1979).
32 Some commentators continue to use the term 'palimony' to describe any property settlement or other financial remedy given to an unmarried cohabitant.
33 See *Marvin v Marvin*, 122 Cal App 3d 871, 176 Cal Rptr 551 (1981).

cohabitation that we cannot impose a standard based on alleged moral considerations that have apparently been so widely abandoned by so many.'[34]

Although *Marvin* is often considered morally radical, it was not particularly transgressive. Women engaged in unmarried cohabitation have been most successful in court when they can show that their relationships followed patterns close to that of a traditional marriage, except for the lack of a ceremony. Typically the women emphasise the family-like sexual division of labour. One view of the California law is simply that it is the sensible treatment of a consensual relationship.

Marvin referred repeatedly to the 'reasonable expectations of the parties'.[35] This raises the question, of course, about what expectations are reasonable. The defendant in *Marvin* may have considered it unreasonable for the plaintiff to expect anything. It is unclear whether men and women in general have similar or systematically different expectations. Some men may expect to enjoy all the benefits of marriage without any of the obligations and to exploit the emotional attachment of their cohabitant for financial gain. Presumably, most courts would conclude that this expectation is not reasonable.

An important question is whether there may be systematic misunderstandings among cohabitants. One study determined that 39% of the unmarried cohabiting couples questioned included one party who fully expected the couple to marry and another who did not.[36] Surely similar miscommunication or differing expectations could be anticipated in terms of their financial relationship. Indeed, even in marriage, many men have no expectation that their increased earning power should be shared with an ex-spouse following divorce. If courts were to require equal sharing of earning capacity following a long-term marriage or cohabitation, there might well be fewer couples in which the woman is encouraged to sacrifice her career possibilities in order to maximise the man's career and job opportunities.

The reasonable expectations of the parties may relate to the subjective communication and power dynamics between that particular couple. The question here would be what interactions between them may have led one or the other reasonably to make certain assumptions. Did one lead the other on, either implying a willingness to care financially for the other, or alternatively implying that the cohabitation would result in no financial obligations? Alternatively, it may refer to a policy judgment regarding what the parties

---

34   Ibid, 18 Cal 3d 660, 683–84, 557 P 2d 106, 831, 134 Cal Rptr 815, 831 (1976).
35   Eg, 18 Cal 3d at 676, 685, 557 P 2d at 116, 122, 134 Cal Rptr 825, 831. See also *Hewitt v Hewitt*, 77 Ill 2d 49, 57, 394 NE 2d 1204, 1207 (1979).
36   See Larry L Bumpass et al *The Role of Cohabitation in Declining Rates of Marriage* Working Paper No 5 at 14 (National Survey of Families and Households, 1989), cited in Lawrence W Waggoner, note 14 supra.

should be assumed to have believed, in the absence of any clear showing to the contrary (by both parties).

There are some potential, generally overlooked, problems with *Marvin*. For example, the threat of a cohabitation suit by someone of the same sex could prove embarrassing to people who have kept their homosexuality secret from many or most people. While it might be assumed that anyone who has actually been cohabiting with a same-sex partner has no secrecy to maintain, it would be quite possible for a room-mate arrangement to have attracted little notice. Although the dissatisfied cohabitant could always breach privacy simply through public statements, the possibility of bringing a lawsuit could seem to make extortion legal and respectable. At some point it might be necessary to choose which is more important to society, fair treatment of people exiting a cohabitation arrangement or the ability of cohabitants to maintain secrecy. These same issues of privacy and extortion arise, though probably in a less compelling fashion, in the case of heterosexual cohabitants.

It should be noted that during the formative period of increased cohabitation, the strongest explanation that couples legally free to marry gave for choosing to remain unmarried was the desire to avoid the legal hassles, and especially the involvement of lawyers, in case the relationship were to break up. It might seem that this reason for avoiding marriage has been thwarted, at least in those cases in which significant amounts of money have accumulated. We lawyers make ourselves indispensable, no matter how hard you may try to keep away from us.

It has been argued that *Marvin* represents an unwarranted State intervention into intimate relationships and thus undermines freedom. It is important to realise that this supposed 'intervention' occurs only when at least one party considers the other to have dealt unfairly. Most unmarried cohabitation ends through agreement and without lawsuit. If both parties deal fairly with each other, they can avoid litigation. Moreover, if they wish to bind themselves to avoid litigation even if they should later find themselves unable to reach amicable or fair agreement, they can do so by a contract such as discussed above. The *Marvin* case is simply the default position for couples who fail to agree to any other arrangement, either before or after their break up. It would be a mistake to believe that the courts' refusal to grant relief to one cohabitant against the other would increase overall freedom in any meaningful way.

II. SUBVERTING MARRIAGE?

Although as many as 20% of the couples cohabiting at any given time are involved in long-term unmarried cohabitation, most people who live with someone they legally could marry either do marry or break up within a fairly short time. Typically in the US, cohabitation either precedes marriage or it is relatively short-term. According to a recent statistic, some 42% of people marrying for the first time cohabited prior to marriage.[37] In the case of second marriage, the percentage of people who cohabited between their first and second marriages rises to about 60%.[38] About 10% of cohabiting couples are still cohabiting, without marriage, in five years' time.[39] Forty per cent of cohabiting households include one or more children.[40]

A major explanation cohabiting couples typically gave to their friends and acquaintances in the 1970s and 1980s when they did choose to get married, was pregnancy or the decision to have children and the wish for the children to avoid the stigma and legal disabilities of out-of-wedlock birth. This major reason given for getting married has been discounted by many courts and rendered largely nugatory by constitutional decisions invalidating most forms of discrimination against children born out of wedlock.[41]

Why should courts refuse to allow parties to avoid lawyers and why should courts pretend that punishing children to control parents is ineffective (as well as unjust)? Are courts merely operating from a totally different experience base and sets of assumptions? A partial explanation emerges from a study of the decisions of the courts. Underlying the field of property division between unmarried cohabitants is the acceptance (and denial) of the double standard of sexual morality. The courts' underlying rationale is actually very crude. Unmarried women involved in sexual relations are either good women who should be married or bad women who should not be able to make demands upon a man beyond whatever he chooses to give her. As they say, prostitutes have to collect before the event.

III. ALTERNATIVE ASSUMPTIONS

During World War II, American military men stationed in England encountered many clashes of cultural understanding with their British hosts.[42] It has been claimed that in the course of a relationship British women interpreted sexual relations as a declaration of engagement to be married, whereas the American men saw it as a sign of loose morals (and potentially a sign of unsuitability for marriage).

---

37   Lawrence W Waggoner, note 14 supra.
38   Ibid.
39   Ibid at 64.
40   Ibid.
41   For the constitutional protection of children born out of wedlock, see Weyrauch et al *Family Law: Legal Concepts and Changing Human Relationships* 743–83 (Minn, West, St Paul, 1994).
42   For a useful description of the effects of the American military presence in Britain during World War II, see David Reynolds *Rich Relations: The American Occupation of Britain 1942–1945* (London, Harper Collins, 1996), esp chap 16, pp 262–283. See also Margaret Mead *Current Affairs* (March 1944) and 'What is a Date?' *Transatlantic* (June 1944).

It may well be that the stereotype of men wanting sex without obligation while women imply an obligation and continuing relationship from the fact of sexual intercourse contains some empirical reality. To the extent this is the case, one could say that the law enshrines or adopts the stereotypically male view of the matter, imposing few obligations upon men who engage in sex. In the case of conception, there may be long-term financial obligations to any child born and not given for adoption, but current law does not impose obligations toward the pregnant woman or mother as such.

There is no reason that the law should not imply from the relationship itself a desire to share – an implied contract for the sharing of lives and money. This could be the 'default position' or the assumption in the absense of a clear agreement to the contrary. While some might argue that a couple who did not intend to share might fail to express their intention in a contract, the same is certainly true of many couples who do intend to share; it seems difficult to argue that it is any more unfair to assume sharing than to assume a choice of no obligation in the absence of contract.

Of greater practical significance, the long history of financial dependence in marriage and the legal enforcement, however inadequate, of sharing upon separation or divorce, encourages certain socially-established scripts and expectations. These include the expectation that a married man will provide the main financial support for the family and that a married woman will provide most of the domestic services, social maintenance and nurturance for the family. She sacrifices the development of her earning capacity for the sake of supporting her family, to maximise the earning capacity of the man, and in order to bear and raise their children. These habits lead to systematic financial inequality between husband and wife.

These scripts often have unexpected and unwelcome effects on couples when they marry. However much they may intend an egalitarian relationship, internal and external pressures lead toward a traditional sexual division of labour. Women do most of the childcare and other unpaid work, while men increase their earning capacity. Indeed, an additional reason couples sometimes give for choosing to cohabit instead of marrying is to reduce the tendency to fall into these patterns. Yet, when cohabitation continues over a period of years, the same pressures that affect a married couple press upon long-term unmarried couples. The existence of established scripts for the behaviour of husbands and wives encourages cohabitation to evolve into an unequal relationship between unmarried 'husbands' and 'wives'.

IV. CONCLUSIONS

One of the interesting criticisms of cases that distribute assets after unmarried cohabitation is that it may leave women better off not getting married than getting married, insofar as a fair and equitable settlement of unmarried cohabitation may be more generous than the property division and support obligations at divorce.[43] This concern would again appear to be based on the assumption that women are and should remain the parties seeking marriage. One can hope that unmarried cohabitation may encourage a rethinking of the fairness or insufficiency of current treatment of assets at divorce.[44] If so, this encouragement of a rethinking may prove to be the most radical and significant legacy of the law of unmarried cohabitation.

---

43 Eg *Marvin v Marvin*, 18 Cal 3d 660, 687, 557 P 2d 106, 123, 134 Cal Rptr 815, 832 (Clark, J, dissenting).
44 See Chapters 1 to 3 supra.